"Tommy offered me the privilege of reading the manuscript of this book shortly after I was diagnosed with metastatic breast cancer. In my sorrow and pain, I was struggling to accept what was happening in my life. Tommy's insight of Ecclesiastes and the wisdom of Solomon is clearly, thoroughly, and perfectly explained. His ability to teach the truth of God's Word displays a deep understanding of God's attributes and the need in man's heart. The book has given me peace and comfort. God's sovereign plan is always for our ultimate good."

— *Sondra McMinn* —
The first person to read this book because of
her circumstances . . . fighting cancer. Again.

"I think this book should be required reading for everyone, especially young adults at the beginning of their lives! All of us, even as Christians, sometimes find ourselves feeling disappointed and disillusioned with life and wondering why things happen the way they do. We strive to find meaning and purpose to our lives, especially in the midst of adversity. This is a book that brings the truth of God's Word alive in a way that helps us discover the true purpose in life, to live as we ought to live, to draw us closer to God, and to rest in His sovereignty over all things. Thanks, Tom, for bringing this message in a way we can all understand!"

— *Eunice Fisher* —
A woman who, all by the age of fifty, lost her first
husband to divorce and her second husband to unexpected
death, and whose third husband now battles Alzheimer's.

The Problem of
Life with God

0-8054-2570-5

Published by Broadman & Holman Publishers,
Nashville, Tennessee

Dewey Decimal Classification: 128
Subject Heading:
BIBLE. O. T. ECCLESIASTES \ SOLOMON,
KING OF ISRAEL \ LIFE

1 2 3 4 5 6 7 8 9 10 06 05 04 03 02

The Problem *of* Life with God

LIVING WITH A PERFECT GOD IN AN IMPERFECT WORLD

TOMMY NELSON

BROADMAN
&HOLMAN
PUBLISHERS

NASHVILLE, TENNESSEE

Dedication

To God the Father Almighty,
"in whose light we see light," who through His saving mercy
made life make sense and yield its delights.

To Teresa,
the wife of my youth, whose love and constant fidelity
has been my joy from the day I met her.

To my father and mother,
who made my growing years the absolute
magic that youth was meant to be.

To the late Howard and Jeanne Tomlinson,
who showed me how to live this book long before I wrote it.
May they rest in peace.

To the saints of Denton Bible Church.
No pastor has borne a sweeter yoke.

AND

To every nook and cranny and cross-street, vacant lot,
baseball field, schoolyard, and buddy in walking distance of
3116 Wenz Street in Waco, Texas—the blessed briar patch of
this brer rabbit that filled my memory with the joy of boyhood.

Contents

CONTENTS

Foreword

Why are we here? Does the Bible answer our most pressing, personal, and painful questions? I believe the answer is yes, and so does Tommy Nelson. *The Problem of Life with God* is a straightforward and insightful look into the Book of Ecclesiastes.

Everyone of us has struggled with the deep questions of life—an untimely death, illness, loss of a job, financial problems, marital problems—all of the questions that cause us to be anxious and many times discouraged in life. This book tells the story of perhaps the only man ever to have everything the world can offer—money, wisdom, and pleasure—and he came to the conclusion that those things cannot satisfy. In this book, Tommy Nelson helps us understand the Bible and how it answers these most personal and pressing questions. It also shows us God's design for our lives.

Perhaps the greatest of all acquisitions is a godly perspective of living—to understand the purpose, meaning, and joy of our existence. This book has done that for me, and I know it can do that for you.

— *Dr. Anthony Evans* —
President, The Urban Alternative
Senior Pastor, Oak Cliff Bible Fellowship

Acknowledgments

Much thanks goes to David Delk, whose skills in writing made this book possible. Also, to Gary Terashita and his confidence and energies in bringing it to light. Thanks to Doug Hudson, who has teamed with me since 1993 to bring God's Word to many hearts through many means. Most of all, to a man I have never met, but whose skill at Bible exposition opened the key to the Book of Ecclesiastes. Thank you, Walt Kaiser.

Introduction

Does the Bible Have Answers for Life's Toughest Questions?

The Book of Ecclesiastes is amazing. It answers some of the most troubling questions we face as men and women.

- Where is God when bad things happen?
- How can I keep from becoming bitter toward God?
- How do I deal with the uncertainty of life?
- What do I do when I'm not sure of God's will?
- When bad things happen, is it because I don't have enough faith?
- Are Christians supposed to have fun?

If you're like me, these questions make you lie awake at night.

As a pastor, most of the heartfelt questions I get asked have to do with what is called the problem of evil: If God is sovereign, He is powerful enough to eliminate evil. If He is good, He would. Since evil clearly exists, God must not be sovereign or He must not be good.

At no point in the history of our country has this question become more real. I finished this book in the aftermath of the events of September 11, 2001. On that day a predator emerged from the jungle like we have never seen before.

Germany in the 1940s industrialized genocide and practiced it on a huge scale. The world responded and defeated this evil. On September 11, 2001, we saw terrorism emerge as an industry. This was the organized and purposeful killing of civilians to create terror. And it was on a scale that dwarfs anything that has come before. Now the world must rise up to stop this evil.

Even so, the specter of September 11 rises like a dark cloud over a God who purports to be both sovereign and good. Where was God on that Tuesday morning? Once again, like when Jesus walked on the water, men are crying out that He is a ghost.

How do we deal with an event as horrendous as the loss of more than three thousand lives and the destruction of those magnificent buildings? Is there any way there could be a purposeful or wise God who would allow such a thing?

Solomon understood that people have questions about God's existence. That's why he devoted two chapters of Ecclesiastes to atheism. But he also understood that those who believe in God will eventually have struggles as well. That's why he devoted ten chapters to the problems we have *with* God.

Solomon answered a basic question about life: How can we live by faith in a world that simply won't behave?

The answers that you will find in this book are the best you are ever going to get. The reason I am so confident is not because I wrote this book, but because this book is simply an explanation of God's wisdom from Ecclesiastes.

Throughout human history, men and women have struggled with the same basic questions. If God made us, it makes sense that He would not leave us in the dark about things that are so important to us. That's why He called Solomon to write the Book of Ecclesiastes.

In Ecclesiastes, Solomon not only dealt with the problem of evil but also with other tough questions in life. These questions have puzzled philosophers and logicians for thousands of years and have probably been troubling you as well. These questions go to the very core of who we are.

Is Ecclesiastes Just a Collection of Random Proverbs, or Does It Have a Deeper Message?

Ecclesiastes is one of my favorite books in the Bible. I love it for many reasons but mainly because it does for life what the Song of Solomon does for love, sex, and romance.[1] Ecclesiastes gives answers to questions that are not answered anywhere else.

Why Solomon?

If ever there was a man who could find meaning outside of God, it was Solomon. In terms of intelligence, industry, and accomplishments, he had it all. Solomon used these gifts to accumulate wealth, discover knowledge, and experience pleasure. And he didn't do it in moderation but excess. If Solomon couldn't discover the secret to life, it can't be done.

Solomon wrote Ecclesiastes at the end of his life. I believe the Song of Solomon was written at the beginning of his life, Proverbs in the middle, and Ecclesiastes after he had failed and repented. This book contains the reflections of a man who played the fool, who had it all and lost it all, and then discovered what was worth having anyway.

In Ecclesiastes, the covenant name of God, Yahweh, is never used. Instead, Solomon refers to God euphemistically by other

---

1. To see how Solomon applies God's wisdom to the areas of love, sex, and intimacy, see my study on the Song of Solomon entitled *The Book of Romance* (Nashville: Thomas Nelson, 1998).

3

references and names. Some scholars believe that this book is written intentionally with the nonbeliever in mind. Ecclesiastes addresses someone who has sincere questions about life and the nature of God. It's a book to the nations. And it is certainly a book for our generation.

In Hebrew, the Book of Ecclesiastes is called *Qoheleth,* or the Preacher. Solomon is not just a philosopher in the sense of a thinker; he takes on the role of God's spokesman to herald what the truth is.

The world's view of wisdom is personified in Rodin's "The Thinker." Biblical wisdom is personified in Solomon, "the Preacher." He's not like so many modern philosophers who pontificate about what might be true; instead, he tells us the facts of life. And these facts instruct us how to live even when faced with continuous disappointment.

A Broad Summary of Ecclesiastes

Solomon begins with the position that life is vain. He does not mean that it is totally meaningless or that it doesn't have any ultimate purpose. By vain, he means that you live for sixty or maybe seventy years and then you're gone. Someone gives away all your possessions and the things that really matter to you are sold for one dollar at a garage sale.

Life just doesn't have any natural reward of itself. It doesn't automatically head to a climactic point of happiness, meaning, and fruition. It just grinds on with the sun rising and setting. Nature never rewards you; instead, it smashes you into pulp, then you die and go into the ground.

All of your possessions that nobody wants end up in a garbage bag. In that sense, man is a vapor and life is vain. A generation comes and goes and you are forgotten. It's like you never existed.

Mark Twain said, "The world will lament you for an hour and forget you forever." Solomon begins with the same observation: Life passes, and instead of rewarding you it grinds you up.

Solomon's Sequential Approach

Solomon systematically works through all of our human attempts to define meaning. The book is not linear, so at first glance to our Western eyes, it does appear to be a random collection of proverbs. But there is a very logical progression to it. Because Solomon is writing from the perspective of an ancient Middle Eastern person, he covers his material by "spiraling" through it instead of moving in a straight line. Still, as we will see, each major section of Ecclesiastes builds on the one before.

Solomon starts Ecclesiastes by describing his efforts at intellectualism. He works through hedonism. Finally he examines materialism.

This process reminds me of so many college students today. During their freshman year, they seek intellectual pursuits and just enjoy the thrill of learning. But by the end of the year, they pledge a fraternity or sorority, then pursue hedonism at full speed for their sophomore year. By the end of that year, they flunk out, repent, go to summer school, come back, and try to learn what they need to know to make a million dollars. That's materialism.

Solomon examines the best thoughts of men and, for every one of them, shows us why they won't work. He proves that in and of themselves these ideas cannot satisfy; they are unable to bring ultimate happiness and meaning to man in his human condition.

Solomon tells us that there is nothing in man that is good. By definition man will have to go outside of himself to find something infinite and whole. In the end, man has to look to God.

And the book doesn't end there—in some ways it gets worse. Someone who believes in God would read the first few chapters and agree with everything Solomon says. The problem is that we will be tempted to quit right there. But then he tells you that just because you're a believer doesn't mean you're not going to have troubles. He shows that bad things happen to the righteous and good things happen to the wicked.

Life is filled with inequality. It can be just as troubling and problematic being a believer in God as being an unbeliever. Even those who believe in God don't end up with all the answers. Instead they often end up puzzled.

Fortunately, Solomon shows us how to make it with a God who doesn't always live up to our errant expectations. In the end, the book is not pessimistic but hopeful.

Solomon ends every section with answers for the questions he has raised. As a matter of fact, Solomon gives the same basic answer seven times. It's a troubling answer, but it's also a simple one. Believe it or not, seven times the answer is to have fun and enjoy the life that God has given.

If you are struggling with the deep questions of life, come with me on a journey into the very heart of man. Read with the eyes of faith, and I think you will see that we are listening to the wisdom of God.

An Outline of Ecclesiastes
Following the Logic of Solomon

I. A Critique of Life: Chapters 1–2
    Life grinds to nothingness, but man keeps searching (1:1–11).
    Intellectualism, hedonism, materialism (1:12–2:11)
    Although wisdom is better, all still die (2:12–16).
    Thus he despaired (2:17–23).
    Conclusion: Apart from God, there can be no life.
               Man in himself cannot find meaning (2:24–26).

II. A Critique of Belief and of Life with God: 3:1–15
     He decrees pain as well as pleasure (3:1–11).
     So enjoy the moment now (3:12–15).

III. The Conflicts of Belief: 3:16–4:16
     Inequity, oppression, rivalry, materialism, and popularity

IV. Be Cautious about Impertinence toward God: 5:1–7
     Be careful how you approach, speak to, and "bargain with"
         our mysterious God.

V.   Be Correct in Perspective: 5:8–7:29
     Wealth: Don't be deceived when the wicked increase; wealth
         won't satisfy (5:8–6:12).
     Adversity: Hard times are not bad; they shape us (7:1–14).
     Yourself: Be humble; you can't know all things (7:15–29).

VI. Be Courageous in Life: 8:1–12:14
     Be bold in doing right even if you're not rewarded
         (8:1–10:20).
     Be bold in living even though you can't control all things
         (11:1–6).
     Be bold in enjoying life although death will come
         (11:7–12:8).

VII. A Creedal Statement: 12:9–14
     God has revealed Himself to us through His Word.

CHAPTER I

The Question
of the Ages

ECCLESIASTES 1:1–18

Where Does Meaning in Life Come From, and Why Does Life Seem So Futile?

Cyril Edwin Mitchinson Joad was born on August 12, 1891, in Durham, England. As a student at Oxford, Joad formed a worldview based on atheism and socialist and pacifist views. Engaged in government service for sixteen years, he retired in 1930 to teach in the departments of psychology and philosophy at the University of London.

As a philosopher, author, teacher, and radio personality, he was one of Britain's most controversial intellectuals of the 1940s. He became famous in Britain as an agile participant in the BBC "Brains Trust" radio program from 1941 to 1947.

An Outline of Ecclesiastes
Following the Logic of Solomon
I. A Critique of Life: Chapters 1–2
Life grinds to nothingness, but man keeps searching (1:1–11).
Intellectualism, hedonism, materialism (1:12–2:11)
Although wisdom is better, all still die (2:12–16).
Thus he despaired (2:17–23).

9

Late in his life, Cyril Joad reversed his course and came to a much different conclusion about reality. To paraphrase him, he said, "I have previously held in my optimism that man would find ultimate good, meaning, peace, and harmony on this earth." He watched with interest the quest of politicians to find peace. He saw the formation of Woodrow Wilson's League of Nations and then the North Atlantic Treaty Organization. But after all was said and done, he also watched men enter into two world wars and kill each other in horrifying ways. In the end he realized that the fundamental problem of man is man.

Cyril Joad repented and accepted the worldview he had formerly rejected. In 1952, he published his final volume, *The Recovery of Belief.*

Cyril Joad's search is a summary of the plight of modern man. People are seeking to understand the world in a way that can give them meaning and wholeness. Sometimes this search is conscious; at other times, it is subtler. But if you look around you today, you will see men and women who, at the core of their beings, are desperate for hope. In our world, hope is the square peg we fumble to fit in the round hole.

Solomon went through this same quest for meaning in 1000 B.C. The Book of Ecclesiastes is as close as the Bible gets to pure philosophy. But it's different from most philosophy in that it is not so much an inquiry of one man's mind as it is God's declaration of the meaning of life.

Solomon's Overarching Lesson: Life in Itself Is Empty

Solomon begins his book by making an observation about life and history.

*The words of the Preacher, the son of David, king in
Jerusalem.*
  "Vanity of vanities," says the Preacher,
  "Vanity of vanities! All is vanity." (vv. 1–2)

In Hebrew, a word is used twice to make it a superlative.
For example, the "holy of holies" means the most holy place. So
when Solomon uses the phrase "vanity of vanities," he means
that life is the ultimate vanity.

When Solomon uses the word "vanity" he doesn't mean
that life is ultimately meaningless. Nor is he saying that life is
chaotic or disordered.

What Solomon means by vanity is echoed in other
Scriptures. As James says, "You are just a vapor that appears for
a little while and then vanishes away" (James 4:14). And God
tells Adam in the Book of Genesis,

*"From [the ground] you were taken;
For you are dust,
And to dust you shall return." (3:19)*

And as Job says,

*"Naked I came from my mother's womb,
And naked I shall return there." (1:21)*

Materially speaking, life is short and then you die. You will
lose everything you own to the next generation. Your children
will rent out your house, purge your possessions, and spend
your inheritance. Ultimately, you will be a distant memory at a
Thanksgiving meal.

Solomon makes what can be a very harsh observation about life: You may want to be immortal but tough luck. You may want to be like King Tut and build a massive pyramid where you can cram all of your precious possessions in the hope that you'll take them with you, but you will go and they will stay. Your best-case scenario is that one day some archaeologist will discover you and your goods, put them in a traveling exhibit, and bring it to Cleveland so children can sneak up and spook each other around your dead body.

You may be a wealthy Indian prince with a devoted wife who throws her body on your flaming funeral bier, but neither your riches nor her spirit will accompany you.

When you die, there will be a funeral. You may have twenty-five or two thousand people attend. But do you know what they'll do after the funeral? They will catch lunch and have a great old time together. Then they will hurry back to work because somebody was covering for them while they took the morning off. That night they'll go home to their families, watch a sitcom rerun, and forget all about your memorial by morning. Are you ready for that?

In the end, you will lose everything. All is vanity. Vanity of vanities—that's life. It goes quickly, you die, and pretty soon nobody knows who you were.

At this point you may be thinking, *Boy, am I glad I bought this book!* Sometimes facing reality is difficult and even discouraging, but that's one great thing about the Book of Ecclesiastes—Solomon tells it like it really is.

In verse 3 Solomon asks a question that begins his explanation of what he means by vanity.

What advantage does man have in all his work
Which he does under the sun?

The word "advantage" literally means "profit." What is a profit? It's what you have left over at the end of the week. It's what you net. When your life is over and you die, what is your profit? You may have enjoyed life and blessed people, but what do you net "under the sun"?

The phrase "under the sun" will be used over and over in this book. It refers to our life here on earth. So when Solomon asks about profit, he is not talking about riches in glory, heaven, or the kingdom of Messiah. Those are truths covered in other biblical books. Solomon is talking about life in this world.

So what profit is there under the sun? In verse 4 he answers that question.

A generation goes and a generation comes,
But the earth remains forever.

You are born into the world, you live your life, and then you die, but the earth keeps right on going. It's like you are walking across a desert, leaving footprints in the sand that the wind erases as though you were never there. Life bankrupts those who invest in it. It mocks those who seek its meaning.

Even the most significant and extreme events are forgotten. Carl Sandburg illustrates this in his poem "Grass."

Pile the bodies high at Austerlitz and Waterloo.
Shovel them under and let me work—
    I am the grass; I cover all.
And pile them high at Gettysburg
And pile them high at Ypres and Verdun.
Shovel them under and let me work.
Two years, ten years, and passengers ask the conductor:

What place is this?
Where are we now?

I am the grass.
Let me work.[2]

The Natural World as a Machine

Also, the sun rises and the sun sets;
And hastening to its place it rises there again.
Blowing toward the south,
Then turning toward the north,
The wind continues swirling along;
And on its circular courses the wind returns.
All the rivers flow into the sea,
Yet the sea is not full.
To the place where the rivers flow,
There they flow again. (vv. 5–7)

In these verses, Solomon describes the natural world as a machine that keeps going perpetually. The sun rises, the winds blow, the rivers flow, and the water evaporates from the sea and rains down from the sky to fill the rivers. Nature is not heading toward a climactic point but is performing an endless cycle of the same thing every day. You can almost hear the "pocketa pocketa" of the cosmic machine's gears and pistons in motion.

As one author said, creation does not leave a residual. It gives no advantage. The earth does not reward you. Entropy is sovereign.

You come, you live, you die, and you go into the earth. The earth does not applaud you—it just keeps going. Man has

2. *Modern American Poetry*, edited by Louis Untermeyer (New York: Harcourt, Brace & Howe, 1919).

always wondered what his purpose is in nature's machine. What meaning can be found in the face of the impersonal cosmos?

Evolution has such a powerful pull on the secular mind because it provides some (albeit unflattering) answers. Evolution answers these philosophical questions by dehumanizing man, proposing that man is nothing but a cosmic accident— a random by-product of the workings of the universe. Hence, man's struggles are caused by his mistaken assumption that there is such a thing as personhood. If man wonders, *Who am I?* evolution answers by eliminating the question altogether: *You are nothing.*

Solomon doesn't try to solve this dilemma of man's ultimate purpose by denying the problem. It's true that in this world, life is nothing but vanity. It doesn't matter who we are because we lose it all. Nobody remembers us. Nobody cares.

Nature is not benevolent. It has no sense of righteousness. If you're good, nature doesn't reward you. You don't start to grow hair in your bald spots when you repent. Nice things don't always happen to you if you are nice to people. Nature is an impersonal machine that consumes you.

Solomon summarized the plight of man in relation to this inhuman, impersonal, destructive, entropy-filled cosmos.

All things are wearisome;
Man is not able to tell it.
The eye is not satisfied with seeing,
Nor is the ear filled with hearing. (v. 8)

Life is tough. Everything is wearisome. Life never resolves into peace and contentment. A man can never stop in his quest for happiness because he will never find it. Our culture is filled with men and women who are destroying themselves to fight a losing battle. They are trying to find happiness in places where it will never be found.

When Solomon says, "Man is not able to tell it," he means that—by himself—man can't figure out life. Man doesn't naturally step back and realize that it's impossible for a finite man in a finite world to have infinite meaning. Man will not say the sum cannot be greater than the parts.

But if the parts are finite and perishable, it should be obvious that life cannot give ultimate meaning in and of itself. If there is any meaning to life, there must be someone outside the system who is infinite and eternal, providing that meaning.

But man is "not able to tell." Man will not stop and declare with resignation, "I can't do it." Rather, our eyes are not satisfied with seeing, nor are our ears filled with hearing. Man in his ignorance will *always* be looking and listening for a new thing. He's like a little gerbil trapped on an exercise wheel, wanting to go faster and faster and faster.

It's been said that man is the only animal that will accelerate when lost. When a person realizes that he can't understand life, instead of saying, "Life is wearisome; I cannot find meaning in this life in and of myself," he just speeds up. He is not satisfied, so he just keeps looking.

Man will always grope for an answer, but look at Solomon's conclusion in verse 9.

That which has been is that which will be,
And that which has been done is that which will be done.
So, there is nothing new under the sun.

Even though man is always looking for something new (i.e., novel, satisfying, and hitherto undiscovered), Solomon says man will never be successful. Anything he tries in the future has already been tried in the past. That which will be done has already been done. Man in and of himself will find no meaning. But he'll always keep scrambling like that gerbil on its wheel— just like the men of Athens who spent "their time in nothing other than telling or hearing something new" (Acts 17:21).

An Overview of History

Let me give you the Tommy Nelson compendium of world history in two pages.[3] In his earliest days, man tried to deify nature. Ancient Canaanite religions personalized the sun and the elements by giving them names. Hinduism called everything god.

Notice that the creation didn't reveal itself. The sun didn't say to ancient man, "Call me Leonard." But man knew that there must be something outside himself that was bigger than he was and could give his life meaning. So by personifying the forces of nature, man gave himself the illusion of being a person—of having morals, intellect, and uniqueness, and dignity.

As nature came more and more under man's control, man slowly but surely began worshiping gods who were like amplified people. Man didn't worship the sea itself anymore; instead he worshiped Neptune or Poseidon. But these gods weren't big enough to last. Man knew that he had to go outside the system and that these gods didn't go far enough.

In about the fifth century B.C., the first philosophers, the Ionians, tried to find something within nature that could give unity and meaning to life. One early philosopher said the unifying force was fire; another said water.

Out of this tradition came Socrates, the first great rationalistic philosopher. He said he didn't know what the answer was,

---

3. For a wonderful overview of the history of thought, see *How Should We Then Live?* by Francis Schaeffer (Grand Rapids: Fleming H. Revell, 1976).

but that it had to be based on reason. His pupil Plato and Plato's pupil Aristotle birthed modern philosophy and the quest to build meaning with reason. They refused to look to the gods and, instead, investigated the fields of knowledge for something to give meaning to everything. This search continued through the Greek- and Roman-ruled periods.

Then Christ came. Now the infinite, personal God became a man who redeemed evil and offered restoration to a fallen world. This was the God who is outside the system; the One who created and sustains the world; the One who made man in His image. The infinite stepped into finitude, eternity stepped into time, and finally everything fit. A fountain of living water was poured into the world.

Then came the fall of Rome, the Byzantine period, and the Middle Ages. The liberating truths of Christ were tainted by legalism and superstition. So men started going on adventures and quests to find hope. They traveled across the oceans to find the city of gold and the fountain of youth. All they found was sin and death.

Then in the Renaissance, men turned back to the Roman and Greek classics and their emphasis on reason. That study didn't bring meaning, but the continuing quest eventually led to the Reformation and the rediscovery of the Bible as the sufficient illustration of faith and practice.

Many great spiritual truths were recovered, but with the rise of the nation-state, rulers became corrupt and oppressed people with their power. So some Christians thought that if they went across the ocean to the New World, they could set up a perfect society. But their utopia didn't work.

With the Industrial Revolution we saw the birth of the modern age and, soon after, the theory of evolution. The generations that followed brought forth philosophic atheism, which proposed that each man was a god. But if we were little gods, you'd think we could do better than to kill each other in two world wars.

In our generation, science has become our god. The pervasive belief is that if we keep discovering new ideas, ultimately we'll find meaning from the universe. But this hasn't worked either.

As nature has failed us once again, we've had a renewed interest in mysticism and irrationality, embracing New Age spirituality and postmodern worldviews. People have even adopted a fascination with extraterrestrials, projecting them as magical beings who have everything under control and can come and fix the mess we've made. People are captivated by extraterrestrials usually because of what amounts to a religious hope, not a scientific inquiry.

Oddly enough, when faced with the coldness of the cosmos, man is not about to turn to God the Father Almighty and His Son, Jesus Christ. If we did that, we would have to acknowledge our need and our sinfulness, so we continue to try other ways to find meaning. In fact, I firmly believe that man's last "hope" will be anti-Christ, who will finally cause man to face his need for repentance in Jesus. And now, back to Solomon and his emphasis: Everything you try to find meaning has already been done.

> Is there anything of which one might say,
> "See this, it is new"?
> Already it has existed for ages
> Which were before us. (v. 10)

No Novel Cure to Man's Ills

The drug culture of the 1960s was not started for the purpose of pleasure or even for getting high. The drug culture started as a response to Eastern philosophy, which promoted a search for meaning deep within ourselves. The opportunity to "drop this and expand your mind" proposed to be something "new."

Remember Timothy Leary, the professor who first advocated drugs to expand consciousness? Interestingly, the whole purpose of the drug culture was to take a trip. But you didn't go to the seven cities of gold, the fountain of youth, or the New World. You expanded your mind to be enlightened. But in the end, drug experimenters found that there was nothing new—nothing to satisfy their search for meaning—in the pills and powders.

Solomon had the answer for them three thousand years ago. You want to be a pantheist? Welcome to India. They were doing it in 2000 B.C. Or is astral projection more your speed? Again, the Indians have been experts in that for centuries. How about Wiccan practices like the worship of mother earth? The Celts were doing it in A.D. 1400. There is nothing new that hasn't been tried before.

Solomon's next verse prophesies man's continual unsuccessful quest for meaning. Man will never learn. He will always repeat his humanistic folly.

There is no remembrance of earlier things;
And also of later things which will occur,
There will be for them no remembrance
Among those who will come later still. (v. 11)

Intellectualism

Solomon offers himself as a living example of this quest for meaning. He goes through three stages—intellectualism, hedonism, and materialism—of pursuing meaning in life and shares his results. His first stop? Intellectualism: the idea that by learning we will ultimately find the answers to give us meaning and peace.

I, the Preacher, have been king over Israel in Jerusalem. And I set my mind to seek and explore by wisdom concerning all that has been done under heaven. It is a grievous task which God has given to the sons of men to be afflicted with. (vv. 12–13)

Solomon says he worked hard to understand life. He says, "I have gone north and south and I have gone east and west. I have gone deep and I have gone broad. I have looked at what the Queen of Sheba has done. I have looked at what the people in India have done. I have looked at what the rich have done. I have looked at every nation we have traded with. I have talked to our sailors and examined every field of wisdom to see if you can find meaning in this dying world."

Solomon says it is a grievous and vain life that we, "the sons of men," have been given. The term "sons of men" literally means the "sons of Adam"—men who have been cursed and are fallen. It is tough to be born a fallen human.

Adam had no philosophic problems in the garden. He walked with God in the cool of the day. He was in touch with infinite reality; he had an absolute answer for creation, for the dignity of man, and for the distinctiveness of his wife. He understood himself in relation to the animals and to the cosmos. He knew why he was here. He knew where he was going. He knew what he was to do, but he sinned.

When Adam sinned, the lights went out. His awareness of his place and purpose vanished. His eyes darkened, and his offspring have continued in that state. His children cannot look up and know what is up above the sun. We're just down here in this machine, trying to find some scrap of meaning. Life is a grief and affliction.

I have seen all the works that have been done under the sun, and behold, all is vanity and striving after wind. (v. 14)

Man in himself—in his finiteness, intellect, pleasure, human religion, and inventions—is grabbing at something that is beyond his reach. The songwriters of my generation contemplated these very thoughts. Consider this verse from Peter, Paul, and Mary's "philosophical" song: "How many roads must a man walk down before he knows he's a man? / How many times do the cannonballs fly before they're forever banned?"

When I listen to Bob Dylan and Peter, Paul, and Mary and a lot of those folks, I realize they weren't singing to make good music because it wasn't that good. They were singing philosophical songs. They were trying to say something. It was the last vestige of hope for my generation. Now nobody cares anymore. Hope has been exhausted. When was the last time you heard about a really good protest? They just don't happen. Those songs of the 1960s were about how men could learn to live with dignity. But, ultimately, their conclusion is the same as Solomon's: "The answer, my friend, is blowin' in the wind."

The answer is blowing in the wind; it remains mysterious and undiscovered. There is nothing new under the sun. All of life is vanity.

The problem is that humans are not capable of altering what's wrong in life. As Solomon points out:

What is crooked cannot be straightened, and what is lacking cannot be counted. (v. 15)

22

This world is fundamentally flawed and you can't fix it. There must be something outside the system that can give purpose to life. Nothing within this universe, you, your abilities, experiences, or mind will give any meaning to life.

It's been said that a good preacher makes points that are bluntly stated, clearly explained, and endlessly repeated. That's what Solomon is doing here.

Mrs. Snodgrass, my English teacher at Waco Richfield High School, would have written "redundant" all over Ecclesiastes with a big red pen. But Solomon knows it will be hard to convince us that knowledge can't bring meaning. He states it again because he really wants us to believe it.

> "Behold, I have magnified and increased wisdom more than all who were over Jerusalem before me; and my mind has observed a wealth of wisdom and knowledge." And I set my mind to know wisdom and to know madness and folly; I realized that this also is striving after wind. Because in much wisdom there is much grief, and increasing knowledge results in increasing pain. (vv. 16–18)

Solomon searched out all of history, sorting through the foolish ideas, good ideas, maxims, and proverbs. He examined the rise and fall of empires. He looked at all the gods and all the religions. He read the important thinkers and had his advisors accumulate as much information as they could. And yet, after all this effort, his conclusion is that it is a striving after the wind. He recognized that he was chasing something he could never grasp. The universe in itself does not contain anything to give meaning, purpose, happiness, joy, and fulfillment in life.

Now the wisdom Solomon is talking about in context is not the wisdom of God and His word; it is wisdom derived from exploring human knowledge—philosophy, religion, psychology, sociology, history, logic, and rhetoric—the best ideas that man has invented or discovered. But in the end, all an educated man can do is die an educated failure. All the learning in the world won't help you change the human heart.

In the movie *Mosquito Coast*, Harrison Ford plays an atheist who flees America to set up a perfect community in a remote jungle. Early in the movie, he meets a missionary (portrayed in the worst light possible) bound for the same area.

When he arrives, the atheist sees immediate success in establishing a thriving village. But by the end of the movie, the atheist totally destroys his village because he finds out that even though he can help people scientifically, he cannot deal with their sinful hearts. And he also finds that he can't deal with his own sin.

Meanwhile the unflatteringly portrayed missionary has a loyal, loving following of people at the end of the movie. Those people are joyful, hopeful, changed, and peaceful—a fact that irritates the atheist. He finally gets so enraged that he destroys everything around him and himself.

When I saw that movie, I said to my wife, "That is Ecclesiastes chapter 1." The atheist increased in wisdom more than all the people around him. He was brilliant. He could change everything about society . . . except the hearts of sinners, so he ended up destroying himself. That is the summary of chapter 1 of Ecclesiastes: You're never going to ultimately change man through human wisdom. Meaning for life must come from something outside of ourselves.

Where have you looked for meaning and purpose? In knowledge? Or success? Or finding the right spouse or having the perfect family? Have you been looking to your career or to money and material things? You are following the "broad path" to destruction that many have trod.

Whatever it is, Solomon has already been there. And his conclusion still stands: Life "under the sun" is emptiness and vanity. There must be something more—a thought that leads us to chapter 2.

For Discussion and Application

1. What does Solomon mean when he compares nature to a machine? What impact does this have on man and our relationship to the world?

2. Has there been a time when you have sped up when you were lost either literally or figuratively? What was that like?

3. Do you think that we have seen a societal shift away from trying to answer deep questions and a move toward just making money and having fun? How has this affected you and those around you?

4. What impact does it have on us when we realize that all meaning must come from outside of ourselves? How does it change our view of ourselves, and how do we deal with this change?

CHAPTER 2

A King's Quest
for Meaning

ECCLESIASTES 2:1–26

Why Do So Many People Believe that Pleasure or Things Will Make Them Happy?

In Stockholm, Sweden, you can spend the night on Lake Malaren in a fifty-nine-room yacht that is a wonderful bed and breakfast. The yacht is a short walk from the Old Town and practically in the shadow of the city hall where the Nobel Prize is awarded each year.

Had you been in Hong Kong on April 26, 1999, you could have bid at the Sotheby's auction for an Imperial family rose cup from the Yongzheng period (1723–35). The cup eventually sold for 17,840,000 Hong Kong dollars.

An Outline of Ecclesiastes
Following the Logic of Solomon
I. A Critique of Life: Chapters 1–2
   Life grinds to nothingness, but man keeps searching (1:1–11).
   Intellectualism, hedonism, materialism (1:12–2:11)
   Although wisdom is better, all still die (2:12–16).
   Thus he despaired (2:17–23).
   Conclusion: Apart from God, there can be no life.
              Man in himself cannot find meaning (2:24–26).

Vigee Le Brun's 1787 oil painting of her daughter Julie is a beautiful example of maternal love and artistic excellence. It is now held in the private collection of Michel David-Weill.

If you would like to charter a private rail car for your next trip by train, Monon's Business Car number three is available. It features a master bedroom with upper and lower berths, a roomette, one fold-down "Murphy" bed, one convertible sofa, a marble tub, a shower, a dining room, meal service, an observation lounge, an open rear platform, a stereo, a television and VCR, cellular and terminal phones, and an all-wood interior.

At this point you may be wondering what these items have in common. Here's the rest of the story.

F. W. Woolworth, founder of the Woolworth's chain of stores, had made one of the largest fortunes in the world by the early 1900s. A portion of this fortune, more than $50 million, was given to his granddaughter, Barbara Hutton, when she turned twenty-one in 1933.

Although she was one of the richest women in America, Barbara was never able to find personal happiness. She married seven times (including among her husbands a prince, a count, and the actor Cary Grant). Hutton spent her life battling drug and alcohol dependency and anorexia, and her numerous divorces left her almost bankrupt. When the reclusive Hutton finally died at age sixty-six, she weighed less than one hundred pounds and only $3,000 of her fortune remained.

What do the four items I mentioned at the start of the chapter have in common? At one time, all of them were owned by Barbara Hutton.

Hedonism

In chapter 2 of Ecclesiastes, Solomon takes us from intellectualism to hedonism.

Many young men and women in America go through a stage in their lives where they believe that if they smoke it, shoot it, drink it, embrace it, and guzzle it, then they will find joy. Often older people never outgrow this pursuit of personal pleasure; we just find more socially acceptable pleasures to pursue in a civilized way. Listen to the wisdom of Solomon.

> I said to myself, "Come now, I will test you with pleasure. So enjoy yourself." And behold, it too was futility. I said of laughter, "It is madness," and of pleasure, "What does it accomplish?" I explored with my mind how to stimulate my body with wine while my mind was guiding me wisely, and how to take hold of folly, until I can see what good there is for the sons of men to do under heaven the few years of their lives. (vv. 1–3)

Solomon pursued pleasure as a lab rat. He stimulated himself with wine, women, and song and took notes. What did he find? Why does pursuing pleasure ultimately end in futility?

Because no matter how much fun you have, at some point you have to wake up to the real world. Pleasure will make you mad or crazy because you have to deny the reality that life is filled with pain. A life based on pleasure doesn't have room for getting fired from a job, seeing a loved one waste away with cancer, or having a child die in a car accident. The only way to live for pleasure is to deny the reality of people hurting all around you with no ultimate meaning and purpose in life. It's madness.

Recently I shared Christ with a young man. He's married and has a couple of sons. He told me he has a group of drinking buddies. Most of them have annihilated their lives and everything good around them. They've lost their families through carousing, adultery, and the pursuit of pleasure.

The young man told me that they had recently asked him to go out. He went with them to a bar where they cranked up the same old music, saw the same women, and drank the same old drinks. He just sat there, thinking, *I've got a wife. I've got great kids who need a good life and education.* Finally he got up and left because he realized he had better things to do.

That man walked out of the bar not because of his Christian morality, but because of Solomon's reasoning. He realized that his buddies' pursuit is vanity; it was madness and useless.

Have you been there? Are you still there? Our affluence in America makes it easy to create a god out of personal pleasure and comfort. Your comfort may not be drinking with your buddies. It may be golf on Saturdays. Or having perfect vacations. Or enjoying fine things in your home. Or watching college sports. Whatever it is, it, too, is futility. If you think there is some pleasure that will make you happy, in the end you will never be satisfied.

Man in his flesh will never cry, "Finis." Man's lusts are like a fire that will never be quenched by any pleasure.

After Hedonism, Materialism

After we wake up to the emptiness in the pursuit of pleasure, we move on to something else. And so Solomon tries accomplishments and career success to bring meaning to life.

I enlarged my works: I built houses for myself, I planted vineyards for myself; I made gardens and parks for myself, and I planted in them all kinds of fruit trees; I made ponds of water for myself from which to irrigate a forest of growing trees. I bought

male and female slaves, and I had homeborn slaves.
Also I possessed flocks and herds larger than all who
preceded me in Jerusalem. Also, I collected for myself
silver and gold, and the treasure of kings and
provinces. I provided for myself male and female
singers and the pleasures of men—many concubines.
Then I became great and increased more than all who
preceded me in Jerusalem. My wisdom also stood by
me. And all that my eyes desired I did not refuse them.
I did not withhold my heart from any pleasure, for my
heart was pleased because of all my labor and this was
my reward for all my labor. Thus I considered all my
activities which my hands had done and the labor
which I had exerted, and behold all was vanity and
striving after wind and there was no profit under the
sun. (vv. 4–11)

Solomon says that he did everything a successful person was
supposed to do. He built and achieved everything he could
want. (Note that "self" is used six times in the previous verses).

He accumulated great wealth in silver and gold. Johnny
Carson once said, "The only value of money is that you don't
worry about being poor." What he meant was that money in
and of itself will not produce anything. It will not help your life,
your marriage, or your kids. As a matter of fact, after a certain
point, money will distract you. Henry Ford once said, "I was
much happier as a mechanic, working in a shop."

Citizen Kane, arguably the greatest movie ever made, illustrates this exact point. In the film, you watch the character
Charles Foster accrue an incredible amount of wealth until it
ultimately destroys him. As Charles Foster is progressively
tainted by his desire for wealth, power, and pleasure, there is a

recurring shot of a fireplace in his home. As the wealth grows and becomes more destructive, the fireplace gets bigger and bigger until in the last few frames, it's the largest thing in the movie.

The fireplace is always burning and consuming. By the end of the movie, the fireplace takes up almost an entire wall of his house. Foster's life is nothing but this raging inferno that never, ever is consumed until he dies.

And when he dies, all his possessions are burned. The viewer watches his entire life go up in smoke.

The only difference between him and most of us is that his stuff produced a lot of smoke. He had a big trash bag. We will have a little-bitty trash bag. But in the end, it all goes up in smoke.

Solomon didn't stop with money. Some people interpret the words in the second half of verse 8 as "instruments" and others as "concubines." Now I enjoy a flute as much as the next guy, but I wouldn't call it the pleasure of men. I think the Hebrew word means concubines. Every pleasure he could conceive of, Solomon tried it.

And his "wisdom stood by" him. He took notes while he was doing it. He investigated every experience to see if it could somehow bring meaning to the vanity of life. Verse 10 shows that Solomon enjoyed the process of building something. But what does he say about the product? "Vanity!"

Solomon's Conclusion

In verse 12 and following, he says, "Here is my reflection."

So I turned to consider wisdom, madness and folly,
for what will the man do who will come after the
king except what has already been done? And I saw

that wisdom excels folly as light excels darkness. The wise man's eyes are in his head, but the fool walks in darkness. And yet I know that one fate befalls them both. Then I said to myself, "As is the fate of the fool, it will also befall me. Why then have I been extremely wise?" So I said to myself, "This too is vanity." For there is no lasting remembrance of the wise man as with the fool, inasmuch as in the coming days all will be forgotten. And how the wise man and the fool alike die! So I hated life, for the work which had been done under the sun was grievous to me; because everything is futility and striving after wind. (vv. 12–17)

Solomon says that he has tried it all and anything else someone does will only be a repetition of what has already been done. There is nothing new. No one is ever going to reach a different conclusion. Solomon has finished gathering the evidence and is giving us a closing statement.

The first thing he says is that it is certainly better to be wise than to be a fool. He says that the wise man has his eyes open and can understand the world around him, while the fool walks around in darkness. Also, it's better to tell the truth than to lie. And it's better to work hard than to be lazy. Would anybody doubt that? It's better to be faithful to your mate than to bring catastrophe to your home. So it's best in life to live wisely and morally.

But what is somewhat surprising is that even though the wise man and the fool may be different in life, they are exactly the same in death. No matter how smart you have been in this life, you're going to die. No matter how moral you have been, you're going to die, and your foolish buddies will die also. And not only will the wise man die just like the fool, he will also be forgotten like the fool.

I was in London a few years ago and went looking for the church of the most famous preacher who has ever drawn a breath in Western civilization. He was born in England in 1834. He became a Christian and preached his first sermon at the age of sixteen. At the age of nineteen he preached as a guest in the famous but mostly lifeless New Park Street Chapel in London. Only two hundred people came to the 1200-seat sanctuary. By the age of twenty-one, he had taken over the full-time pastorate of this historic congregation.

Within a year, New Park Street Chapel had to be enlarged to seat the crowds who came to hear him preach. Yet still more people came to hear him preach, so in 1861 the church moved into the Metropolitan Tabernacle which could accommodate sixty-five hundred people. His sermons were so popular that a publisher printed and sold one sermon each week for more than twenty-seven years. This preacher not only started orphanages to care for thousands of children but he also influenced the lives of businessman, government officials, and kings.

His name was Charles Haddon Spurgeon. When he died in 1892, Spurgeon was perhaps the most famous man in the world.

So when I went to London, I wanted to see his church. I found the right area of town and started asking a few locals if they could show me the way to Mr. Spurgeon's church.

Guess what they said? "Mr. Who?" I found out that I, a small-town Texas boy, knew infinitely more about Charles Haddon Spurgeon than these guys from London. They didn't have a clue!

The foolish and the wise both will be forgotten. As Wordsworth wrote, "Our hearts like muffled drums, beat funeral dirges to the grave." A college professor of mine used to say, "When a child is born, another death is brought into the world."

The world consumes you. Solomon comes to the same conclusions in 1000 B.C. that modern man reaches. It's like looking through a time tunnel. He foresees what is to come. He's saying to all of the Greeks and the Romans, to all the Englishmen and the Westerners, to Hume the Scotsman, to Voltaire the Frenchman—this is where you will end up. If you try to find finite things to give you meaning, your search will end in vanity. Solomon is a 1000 B.C. man with twentieth-century depression.

> *Thus I hated all the fruit of my labor for which I had labored under the sun, for I must leave it to the man who will come after me. And who knows whether he will be a wise man or a fool? Yet he will have control over all the fruit of my labor for which I have labored by acting wisely under the sun. This too is vanity. Therefore I completely despaired of all the fruit of my labor for which I had labored under the sun. When there is a man who has labored with wisdom, knowledge and skill, then he gives his legacy to one who has not labored with them. This too is vanity and a great evil. (vv. 18–21)*

Solomon says that he ended up hating the things he had built and accumulated because he knew that he could not take them with him. He was going to have to leave them in the hands of someone who would follow him. Note his progression: He hates his labor, then he completely despairs. Solomon is depressed. This is the inevitable ending of a life without God.

Solomon is humanity in a microcosm. A life built on self heads toward depression and despair.

It is also the story of F. W. Woolworth and Barbara Hutton. Solomon says that when you work hard to make a fortune, build an empire, and be a success, you're still going to die. And when you do, you will leave everything behind. Barbara Hutton received a magnificent yacht for her eighteenth birthday. Today you can book a room in that yacht in Stockholm for $59 a night.

Someone will end up with your big, pretty Rolls Royce and spill coffee all over its polished wood. Someone will take your beautiful house, paint it orange, and rent it to a bunch of college freshmen. Your favorite pair of $200 shoes will end up at the Salvation Army. The land that is so precious to you will end up as a trailer park in fifty years. It's the same for the wise man and the fool—you can't take it with you when you're gone. All lives lead to a casket.

> *For what does a man get in all his labor and in his*
> *striving with which he labors under the sun? Because*
> *all his days his task is painful and grievous; even at*
> *night his mind does not rest. This too is vanity.*
> *(vv. 22–23)*

Even while you are alive and enjoying the things you accumulate, they are still a pain. The more things you have, the more things you have to take care of.

Solomon says that as hard as you work during the day, at night you will lie there and worry. You aren't going to lie down to sleep and think, *Happy am I. Behold my car. Behold my house. Behold my trophy wife.* Instead, you twist and flap in the stress and trouble that come with your accumulated glories.

At this point, Solomon is using a literary device. He is building tension and anticipation. You are *meant* to be depressed when you read this. Solomon is letting the tension build before he provides the answer.

There is nothing better for a man than to eat and
drink and tell himself that his labor is good. This also
I have seen, that it is from the hand of God. (v. 24)

It's unfortunate that there is a textual problem in this verse because it may be the crux of the whole book. Now I don't know Hebrew at all, but I read the guys who do. Walt Kaiser, who I believe wrote the best commentary ever on Ecclesiastes (*Ecclesiastes: Total Life*, Moody Press), says that the word "better" is not there in Hebrew. Because it is used in other places in the book, translators have considered it to be implied and have added it.

But Kaiser suggests that this is a mistranslation of the text. It should read: "There is nothing in man to eat and drink and tell himself his labor is good."

That fits perfectly with what Solomon has said in the first two chapters. Wealth, pleasure, knowledge, accomplishments—there is nothing "in man" that he can learn or do that can give him happiness or peace. Man can find nothing in this finite life to give him an infinite peace. Man must go outside of himself or he will live his life in despair. The only way a person can avoid this is by living in denial.

Solomon Gives Us the Answer
For who can eat and who can have enjoyment without
Him? (v. 25)

Solomon says that the only way we can find real enjoyment and meaning in life is by getting in touch with something infinite. God has to come to us and give us something that we don't have. Man under the sun—man doing it on his own—will inevitably end in despair, futility, and death. If we are ever going to find something that is good, we'll have to get it from the hand of God.

This is called grace. And to experience it, you have to look up. You have to lift your eyes to heaven to find meaning. There is no happiness in life without God.

Have you discovered that? A lot of us, even though we know it at one level, still don't really believe it. Instead we look at God as our Sunday buddy. Or we treat Him as a genie who will magically appear when we're in trouble. Or we try to have a partnership with Him: "God, come in. You can have this part, but I'll handle these other things myself."

In verse 26, Solomon shows that it's not enough to believe in God intellectually; we also need to be someone who is good in His sight.

> *For to a person who is good in His sight He has given wisdom and knowledge and joy, while to the sinner He has given the task of gathering and collecting so that he may give to one who is good in God's sight. This too is vanity and striving after wind.*

What does the Bible say is the beginning of wisdom? The fear of the Lord (Ps. 111:10). For the man who fears God, the lights come on and he sees life correctly. Not only that, but he has knowledge and true joy. All this comes to someone who obeys Him, submits to Him, loves Him, and seeks Him. And ultimately, when the final accounting is done, the things that have been accumulated by the wicked will be taken by God and given to those He has made righteous through Christ.

Back to Adam: He was perfectly happy in the original creation because he knew God. He sinned, and suddenly his descendants were blinded to God, themselves, creation, evil, maleness, femaleness, and children. They lost sight of God and couldn't understand life. And we are still arguing about defining and appreciating these things today because so many people in our culture are in the dark and can't see. If you don't know God, you can't know anything He made.

What is the most important verse in the Bible? That's easy. It's Genesis 1:1—"In the beginning God . . ." If you want to understand reality, you have to start with God.

In the 1960s, there was an American girl attending college in Switzerland. At the school she met a lot of young postmodern Europeans. They were steeped in philosophy, humanism, atheism, and nihilism, and some of them doubted that they even existed. They had no reference point—other than their own emotions and insight—to make sense of the world. They didn't know that they were looking for something infinite.

In contrast, this American girl had no problem intellectually with the questions she faced. Her friends asked her why she seemed so content. She said, "Because I believe that the infinite, personal God made us, and we're not simply part of nature. We are created in the image of God. Evil is not just something out there that looks unpleasant; it is truly evil because it's contrary to Him. God has made Himself known in the Bible. The paramount idea of the Bible is the person of Jesus Christ who came to save us from sin. Through Him we can know God and enjoy everything He has given. We can die in hope."

They asked her where she learned these things. She told them she had learned them from her father. So they came to her house and her father, Francis Schaeffer, began to show them how their worldview ultimately ended in despair. A few of these young people trusted Christ, and soon people from all over the world were coming to *L'Abri,* "the shelter."

Hundreds of searching young men and women found rest from a transplanted American who knew God. As a matter of fact, his ministry got so big, he quit everything else. He did nothing but work with these twentieth-century modernistic guys. With patience, wisdom, and the power of the Spirit, he brought them to the knowledge of God and to the knowledge of life through Jesus.

That's the answer for each of us. Again, if you don't know God, you don't know anything that He made. If you know Him, the whole world lies open before you. "A scoffer seeks wisdom and finds none, / But knowledge is easy to him who has understanding" (Prov. 14:6).

For Discussion and Application

1. Why do you think man is so tempted to find meaning in pleasure? Have you ever tried this or been close to someone who has? What eventually causes someone to move beyond this method?

2. Johnny Carson said, "The only value of money is that you don't worry about being poor." Do you agree or disagree? How are you affected by the materialistic mind-set of America? Have you ever given in to the idea that some thing will make you happy? If you are studying this book with a group and feel comfortable, share a specific example.

3. Why is the interpretation of verse 24 important? How does Walt Kaiser's suggestion make the verse fit in the context? How does this square with your experience?

4. Verse 26 suggests that the sinners are working to hand over their goods to the righteous. Do you see that happening in your experience? What do you think Solomon means?

5. If you don't know God, you don't know anything that He made. If you know Him, all of life is open to you. Do you agree or disagree? Is this statement too extreme? How does knowing God help us understand the true nature of the world around us?

CHAPTER 3

The Problem *with* God

ECCLESIASTES 3:1–15

Why Do Bad Things Happen to Me When I Love God and Am Trying to Do the Right Thing?

If I had written the Book of Ecclesiastes, I would have stopped at the end of chapter 2. It would have been a very, very short book. It would have been like 2 John, Jude, or Philemon.

Solomon has written a wonderful conclusion—for any person to find ultimate meaning in life, he has to go outside of himself to God. Sounds like a great way to end a book to me. Let's close with a rousing hymn and go home.

But there are another ten chapters to the Book of Ecclesiastes. Solomon kept writing because he knew we would have a problem with God. In some ways, we'll have as much of a problem *with* God as we had *without* Him in the first few chapters. That's something I love about the Book of Ecclesiastes: Solomon is brutally honest.

An Outline of Ecclesiastes
Following the Logic of Solomon
II. A Critique of Belief and of Life with God: 3:1–15
   He decrees pain as well as pleasure (3:1–11).
   So enjoy the moment now (3:12–15).

A little girl in my church is named Sally. She was marvelous at ballet. She was beautiful, smart, and about nine years old when her life took a harsh turn. She went up to visit her grandparents in the Midwest one time and after she arrived, she started running a fever, then had a seizure and kept having them all night long. The doctors said they had to stop her seizures or she would die, so they put her in a coma. They waited and then slowly brought her out of it, but the seizures began again and have never been brought completely under control.

Now that beautiful, intelligent, talented little girl has permanent brain damage. Her parents, who love the Lord, have to watch Sally grow up. She's through with ballet. She cannot attend the same school. She looks at you with eyes that seem to be hunting for something to connect with. What would you say to her parents?

I know another man who is a spokesman for a Christian organization and has served God all of his days. He had a son that wandered from the faith and got in trouble. For years, he prayed and prayed and prayed for his son and lived with the consequences of his son's actions; finally his son surrendered his life to Jesus Christ.

Not long after that, his son was going to work one morning on his motorcycle when he crossed an intersection, got hit, and was killed immediately.

This committed Christian man—the boy's father—cried out in his pain to God, saying something that he never thought would come out of his mouth. He said, "God, I take better care of Your children than You do of mine." He shared his honest feelings about the tragedy with God.

If we want to deal with the world as it really is, we are going to have problems with God. When bad things occur, what are your solutions? Do accidents really happen to people? Is Satan

44

the cause of every bad thing in the world? How would you answer these questions?

Solomon shows that no matter how you slice it, the sovereignty of God lies behind everything that happens. The existence of evil is one of the great philosophical problems of all time: How did evil come into existence from an all-holy God?

In many ways Satan is sometimes easier to understand than God. Satan in a sense is very simplistic. He is a being of pure evil. That means his reasons for doing everything he does are easily understood.

God, however, is a problem. It's often difficult to interpret His actions in the short-term. If He's good and all-powerful, why is there so much suffering in the world?

It's this problem with God that Solomon tackles in Ecclesiastes 3.

There is an appointed time for everything. And there is a time for every event under heaven— (v. 1)

Solomon says that however we try to resolve the fact that evil exists and God is good, we can't do it by saying that God is not in control. In this section Solomon clearly states that God has a plan and does not waver from it. He is the one who has made the appointed time for everything. Solomon was a Calvinist long before there was a Calvin.

Entire books are devoted to just this subject of predestined activity in life, so we can't give it full treatment here. I will choose to affirm what the Bible affirms. God is sovereign over everything. He is not always pleased, but He is never perplexed. No evil action skirts His plan. No piece of the puzzle is left over at the end. Either God is sovereign or He is not. Solomon goes on to reiterate and explain his point.

Every Event Is Part of God's Plan

A time to give birth, and a time to die;
A time to plant, and a time to uproot what is planted.
A time to kill, and a time to heal;
A time to tear down, and a time to build up.
A time to weep, and a time to laugh;
A time to mourn, and a time to dance.
A time to throw stones, and a time to gather stones;
A time to embrace, and a time to shun embracing.
A time to search, and a time to give up as lost;
A time to keep, and a time to throw away.
A time to tear apart, and a time to sew together;
A time to be silent, and a time to speak;
A time to love, and a time to hate;
A time for war, and a time for peace. (vv. 2–8)

Solomon says it doesn't matter if you're a man or a dandelion, there is a purpose for your birth, your death, and everything in between. God has appointed a time for everything that happens.

A day will come in God's sovereign plan when you will receive a phone call telling you that your parents are dead. Your time will be to weep. But it won't last forever because there will be a time when you will get a big promotion or finally move into your dream home, and then you will laugh.

Solomon says life is going to be like this and there is absolutely nothing you can do about it. You'll have children and you will laugh. Then one day you'll cry because of those children. That's the way it is. There are times of happiness and times of pain. If you don't die from something unexpected, there will be a day when you will weep over some diagnosis. All of these things are ordained. We cannot know what life will bring.

46

There is a time that you destroy something by throwing stones, but there's also a time that you gather stones to build something. There will be a time for you to embrace, but there will also be times when you don't want anyone around.

There will come a time that you will be full of hope and will want to search. There will also be a time when you will be hopeless and want to give up. The things you own will be useful for a while, and you will want to keep them. But one day you will take your stuff to Goodwill; it's time to throw it away.

There will be a time for agony. You will hurt so bad, you will want to tear your clothes. And then there will be a time to sew up the tears because the pain is gone. There will be times when you will want to keep your mouth shut and times when you just have to tell somebody something.

There'll be a time for love. There will also be a time of rejection.

That's a fact. All of these things are appointed.

Solomon says that God is not your genie. God does not cooperate with us the way we think He should. He doesn't behave. As was said of Aslan in the Chronicles of Narnia, "He is not a tame lion." And when we realize this, it leads us to a very human response.

What profit is there to the worker from that in which he toils? (v. 9)

We say to ourselves, "Why should I work so hard when it's all going to be destroyed? Why get married when you just end up fighting and hurting one another? Why have a child and deal with the stress and disappointment? Why should I go on living when I know at some point I'm going to get the twenty-four-hour stomach flu?"

Personally, I'd rather die than have the stomach flu. Don't you just love waking up disoriented at 3 A.M. and being sick for about forty-five minutes straight? Guess what? Your lucky bout with it is coming!

Solomon is playing the devil's advocate here. He is saying what all of us think and sometimes wish we could say. What profit is there? Everything gets undone and it's all been ordained anyway. It is easy to get cynical.

Do you ever feel like that? What's the use? Why not punt? Solomon put this into perspective.

> *I have seen the task which God has given the sons of*
> *men with which to occupy themselves.*
> *He has made everything appropriate in its time.*
> *He has also set eternity in their heart, yet so that man*
> *will not find out the work which God has done from*
> *the beginning even to the end. (vv. 10–11)*

In the first two chapters of Ecclesiastes, Solomon tells us that there is no hope unless we turn to God. Now we have a bigger problem because we have turned to God. We find out that He has given us this life of vanity and toil. He has appointed everything that happens in our lives.

How do you live in a world that is out of your control? How do you live with a God who doesn't always make sense? Again, the Hebrew translation of "sons of men" in verse 10 is "sons of Adam," reminding us of the fallen state of man. It's just hard to be a fallen man in a fallen world.

The Four Platforms

From verse 11 to the end of chapter 3, Solomon gives us four platforms that can help us stand. The first one is that God's plan is wise. *God is wise,* and even bad things have a purpose. He makes everything appropriate or beautiful in its time.

When an appointed thing occurs, it may not seem that it has any purpose whatsoever, but God sees it from a totally different perspective.

I was teaching this idea in our church and had asked Norma, a wonderful pianist, if she would play for the congregation. I asked her to play "Jesus Loves Me" using only the white keys. When she played, it had a very simple sound. Frankly, it wasn't very interesting.

Next I asked her to play it using as many black keys as she wanted. If you've ever played a piano, you know that by themselves the black keys don't sound very good. That's where all the sharps and flats are. But when Norma played "Jesus Loves Me" and included the black keys, it created a lush, beautiful sound. I asked my congregation to vote on whether they liked it with the white keys only or with the black keys added in. Without a doubt, the song sounds better with the black keys.

Life is just like a song played on the piano. It is a caricature without the black keys. It's not heroic without sin, evil, and pain. You don't know or appreciate the heroism, love, and patience of God until evil enters the world.

I enjoy a good movie, and one of the most interesting and unique movies I've seen in a long time was *The Truman Show* with Jim Carey. I went to see it with my wife and son and did not know anything about the plot before the movie started. After about fifteen minutes of watching the movie, I leaned over to my wife, Teresa, and said, "Something's wrong here." Everything going on in the movie was perfect—no difficulties to move the plot forward—and it was obvious that Jim Carey was overacting. Frankly, it was boring.

Then a few things start to unravel, and you find out why his life is perfect. Ed Harris's character has contrived this world for Truman where there is no evil and nothing bad can happen to him. But there is also no heroism, no real friendship, no real love, no virtue, and certainly nothing worth living for. Ultimately, Truman refuses to live in this "perfect" world any longer.

That's what life would be like if you didn't have black keys.

The parts of our lives that don't feel right at the time are woven together by God to form a beautiful tapestry. God's plan is wise—it's just that He doesn't ask you and me for our opinions. There is no suggestion box in the tabernacle. We have to trust Him.

When I was eleven years old, one of the most tragic incidents in my life happened. If you have ever been involved in Little League baseball, you know that there is almost nothing more important than making the cut as an eleven-year-old All-Star. I was not selected for the team, and what's worse, two of my eleven-year-old buddies were. I was utterly devastated.

My mother sat down with me on my bed and said, "Let me tell you a story." She told me about a guy in the Bible who had a promise from God that he would be a ruler. But he was thrown in a pit and sold into slavery. Then he was thrown into jail and forgotten. Through all of his disappointments, he kept doing the right thing because he believed in trusting God's promise. Later when Joseph looked back on those harsh experiences, he saw that God used them to get him in a position to save his family.

My mother said to me, "Tommy, there will be a lot of times in your life when God does things that don't seem to have any rhyme or reason whatsoever. You've got to trust Him even when

He doesn't give you the answer." Pretty good counsel, wasn't it? Believing that God is wise is the only thing that will sustain you when He plays your life on the black keys.

Solomon shows us that not only is God's plan wise, but *it is also mysterious*. Solomon says in verse 11 that God has one plan from beginning to the end. He doesn't react to the devil's activities as though a cosmic tennis match is being played.

It's not as though God created man, then Satan tempted him. Then God decided to kick man out of the garden. So Satan caused Him to corrupt civilization. Then God countered with a flood . . . and so on.

No, God has a plan like a Beethoven sonata, beautifully intermingling white keys and black keys. The white keys by themselves are boring. The black keys by themselves are troublesome. When you put them together, they're lovely.

Still, there is mystery. God put eternity in the heart of every person, and in every person is the question *why*. All through the Bible we see men of God ask why bad things are happening. Habakkuk says,

Why hast Thou made men like the fish of the sea,
Like creeping things without a ruler over them?
(1:14)

He is asking God, "Where are You?"

Jeremiah says to God,

Why has my pain been perpetual
And my wound incurable, refusing to be healed?
Wilt Thou indeed be to me like a deceptive stream
With water that is unreliable? (15:18)

Jeremiah is saying to God, "You promised, and it sure seems like You are not there."

Have you ever wondered where God was or whether He cared? Why do we ask those questions? Because He has set eternity in our hearts. We intrinsically know that there has to be some order and purpose to life.

So even though we can recognize God's work or purpose in some things, we squint our eyes and try to figure out all the things we can't see. We ask questions like, "Why was I born this way? Why did my father treat me that way? Why did You take my friend? Why am I missing out on this blessing?" We squint but we can't see. He's put eternity in our hearts but won't give us all the answers.

As one author said, "There is a deep-seated, compulsive drive to transcend our mortality by knowing the meaning and destiny of life."

It's troublesome. We want to see the future outcome of problems and say, "So that's why You let this happen to me." But God says, "I'm sorry, I'm not going to show you." He does things in our lives that are not pleasing or pleasurable, but they are wise. Solomon says we have to trust Him.

God is wise but He is also mysterious. In verse 12 we see Solomon's third platform for life.

I know that there is nothing better for them than to rejoice and to do good in one's lifetime.

Solomon wants to tell us that even when we don't understand everything God is doing, *we cannot let what we cannot know destroy what we can enjoy.* You can't be God and control circumstances. There's nothing you can do about that. So don't let it negate your present enjoyment of life.

Every week I counsel Christians who are upset because they are not God. I see the torment they experience because they can't deal with their helplessness and confusion. But the truth is that they've *never* been able to understand everything that was occurring, good or bad. So what should we do?

Solomon tells us not to get cynical and unhappy; instead, we should do good in our lifetime. In this short life you have to trust God and do good. And in verse 13, Solomon says life does not have to be meaningless.

Moreover, that every man who eats and drinks sees good in all his labor—it is the gift of God.

John Piper wrote a great book called *Desiring God: Meditations of a Christian Hedonist.* That title may make you nervous, but I love it. I love it because there is a blessedness in seeking pleasure the way God intended. We are to enjoy pleasure.

Everyone is going to die. As you read this book, the clock is ticking. The twenty-four-hour virus is waiting on you. There are germs on your teeth that will cause cavities. One day you'll have to have a root canal. All of those things are bad and they are coming.

So today, while everything's OK, go get a double dip of Rocky Road ice cream (or whatever flavor you favor) in a waffle cone. Take some friends with you, lick your ice cream slowly, and just enjoy being together. Call an old friend you haven't spoken to in six months and get caught up. Rent a movie you've wanted to see and curl up on the sofa with some hot popcorn.

Jesus put it like this: "Do not be anxious for tomorrow; for tomorrow will care for itself" (Matt. 6:34). Enjoy today—trust God and have fun. We all know that you'll eventually have that virus, and that root canal is so certain that it may as well already be scheduled, and one night you'll receive a phone call telling you your father has passed on. So today you need to go get your two dips of Rocky Road.

I like that. I don't know what my life holds. Some day, a doctor may look up from his chart and tell me he found something that shouldn't be in me. I'll get cut, burned, and poisoned with a cancer treatment and I'll be pretty miserable. But today I'm doing OK. So I'm going to get together with some good buddies and enjoy our conversation.

On Wednesday night, I've got a date. Maybe I'll take my wife to get some Italian and order some chicken parmigiana. I'll talk to my lovely wife and eat that good food and afterward, I'll get a little cheesecake and a cup of coffee. It will be wonderful. Maybe there'll be a little Johnny Mathis playing in the background.

I know the day is coming when they'll find something in me, or some car will cross the yellow line and hit me head-on, or this body will just wear out. But I refuse to let what I can't control destroy what I can enjoy. The third platform that we can stand on is to chill out and enjoy life while we can.

The final platform is to *rest in the sovereignty of God*. Look at what Solomon says in verse 14.

> *I know that everything God does will remain forever;*
> *there is nothing to add to it and there is nothing to*
> *take from it, for God has so worked that men should*
> *fear Him.*

God's sovereignty is not meant to trouble us; it is meant to comfort us. Whenever anything horrible happens, there is only one thing I have to know: God is in control. His plan is unchangeably perfect.

If I left my office today and found out my wife had died, I would be devastated and I would mourn, cry, and wail. And you know what? God would not tell me why. He refuses to explain Himself to us.

But I do have to know one thing—and if I can't be sure of this I don't want to go on. I have to know that He is in charge and that His plan is good.

I have no problem with God allowing things that do not fit in my framework because I know I am a fool. But I will not live in a universe that is run by evil. If God is that weak, then I will crawl into bed and pull the covers up and never come out.

Have you ever been repelling off the top of a cliff, where you turn, walk backward to the edge of the cliff, and then jump? Before you jump, you don't just whistle to any handy bystander and say, "Hey, buddy, can you come here and hold this rope?" No, you find someone you trust who will make sure you and the rope are secure, then you jump.

Solomon tells us in verse 14 that everything God does will remain forever. He is not shortsighted and wondering how it will all work out.

He also says there is nothing to take away from what God has done. There is no red ink on God's decree. You don't add to it and you don't take away from it: it's perfect.

And the goal is that men would fear Him. God is not trying to produce cynicism, but reverent fear. He wants to create trust in us. Mystery shouldn't repel us; it should make us bow.

That which is has been already, and that which will be has already been, for God seeks what has passed by.
(v. 15)

Everything that is happening now has been decreed in the past. Everything in the future will happen according to plan.

And God seeks or fulfills what is lost from a human point of view. In other words, in God's wise arrangement of events, He can call back (seek) the past and connect it with the future.

It's like when you work on a jigsaw puzzle and have one piece that just stumps you. So you set it aside and work on the rest of the puzzle. At some point you find a perfect place for your piece and you *seek what has passed by.*

God is perfect. Even though there are events in your life that don't make sense right now, when it's all said and done, God will seek what has passed by. He will insert that piece of the puzzle that finishes the whole picture. Painful and bad things happened in my life, but later on, God sought what passed by. Then I said, "Aha!"

In *The Hiding Place,* Corrie Ten Boom gives a wonderful example of this truth. She and her sister Betsy were being held in a concentration camp. Betsy said that they still had to trust God and thank Him for everything.

We're talking hard-core Christianity. Everything about the camp was awful—being in the middle of a war, being separated from family, and watching other prisoners die. But day in and day out, the things that Corrie hated above everything else were the lice that bit her in bed. It was miserable. She couldn't get away from them. It was impossible to get a good night's sleep.

One time when Corrie and Betsy were thanking God for everything, Betsy interrupted Corrie at the end of her prayer and said, "And the bedbugs, Corrie—thank God for those lice." Corrie thought her sister was crazy, but she thanked God for bedbugs by faith.

After they had been at the camp a few days, they started a Bible study in their barracks—an unauthorized activity that would've provoked the guards. But the guards never came into their barracks to break up the study or order them to quit. They always wondered why.

Later Corrie learned it was because the guards were afraid of catching the lice.

It turned out that the shield of God around Corrie and Betsy Ten Boom was a bedbug. Do you see how God seeks what passes by? Only God could use a bedbug!

Again, these are Solomon's four platforms: *God is wise; God is mysterious; enjoy today; and rest in the sovereignty of God.*

Another thought also helps me deal with the evil I can't explain. The greatest act of "injustice" that has ever happened took place about two thousand years ago. The only perfect person who ever lived, the divine man, was rejected, betrayed, denied, tortured, put on a cross, and killed. He, of all people, didn't deserve any of it.

Jesus was the one person who did everything God required of Him. He did not fail or err in a single point. And what did He get for all His obedience and righteousness? He got tortured and nailed to a cross to suffocate to death. What good could possibly come out of an evil like that?

Yet God turned the most evil thing that has ever happened into the best thing that has ever happened. Today we can *celebrate* Jesus's suffering and death because He triumphed over sin and rose from the grave. For three days, it didn't make sense. On the third day, everything became clear. Jesus had been "delivered up by the predetermined plan and foreknowledge of God" (Acts 2:23).

No matter what you are going through right now, you have not faced anything like Calvary. The purpose of that evil experience was so you and I could be secure in heaven. Now if God can do that, can't He take your situations and use them for His good? Will He explain it all to you? He will not.

God doesn't promise that there will be a "third day" when we will understand all the bad things that have happened in our lives. But He does give us the promises we need to place all our trust in Him.

He requires one thing of you in the face of this uncertainty: Don't let what you can't control destroy what you can enjoy.

For Discussion and Application

1. Do you agree that there are no easy answers to explain God's allowance of painful events? Why or why not?

2. What is the first of the four platforms Solomon gives us? Why is it important that life is also "played on the black keys"?

3. What is the second platform? Why does God make us want to know why and then not provide the answers?

4. What is the third platform? How have you applied this truth to your life in the past? How can you take this truth to heart today?

5. What is the fourth platform? How does the death of Christ serve as an example of this truth?

CHAPTER 4

Living in
an Insane World

ECCLESIASTES 3:16–4:16

How Can I Trust God
When the World Is Filled with Injustice?

In 1947, Simon Wiesenthal formed a volunteer organization to help find and prosecute Nazi war criminals. During the next forty years, Wiesenthal's organization helped track down more than one thousand war criminals, including Fritz Stangl, the former commandant of the Treblinka death camp.

What was Wiesenthal's motivation? He had plenty of good reasons. During World War II, he spent the last three years of the war in a series of labor and concentration camps. The Nazis killed eighty-nine members of his and his wife's Jewish families during the war. But when asked the reason for his work, he pointed to one concrete experience that happened in a World War II death camp.

One day two Nazi officers rode to the site where the prisoners were excavating rock. One of them grabbed a Jewish

---

An Outline of Ecclesiastes
Following the Logic of Solomon
III. The Conflicts of Belief: 3:16–4:16
  Inequity, oppression, rivalry, materialism, and popularity

man and made him stand back to back with another Jewish man. He had a guard bind the two men together with ropes. Then, just as calmly as if he were swatting a fly, he pulled out his gun and shot through the first man's head into the head of the man behind him, killing them both with one bullet. He turned to the other officer and said, "See, I told you we've been wasting 50 percent of our bullets."

Simon Wiesenthal's response to the atrocities he experienced was the assertion that "God is on leave."

At the beginning of their experience in the concentration camps, Betsy Ten Boom said to her sister, "Corrie, we are in hell."

Have you ever been through a time of suffering which seemed to have no possible redemptive purpose? That's why I love the Book of Ecclesiastes. It is far more honest about life than we are sometimes.

In this chapter, Solomon tackles more than just the random pain and suffering we experience. In verse 16 and following, we see that the plan of God also includes inequity and even insanity sometimes. When these insane things occur, you, like Wiesenthal, believe that He must be on leave. Or like Betsy Ten Boom, you feel that you are in hell and He's nowhere to be found.

In verse 16, Solomon uses the term "I have seen." Again in verse 22 he says, "I have seen." In 4:1 he says, "I looked again"; 4:4, "I have seen"; 4:7, "I looked again"; and in 4:15, "I have seen."

Solomon knows that his conclusion is going to be hard for us to accept, so he wants us to know that he has observed it long and hard. Over and over, Solomon shows us what he has witnessed about the insanity of life in the context of a sovereign God. God has rigged life so that we have to trust Him even though it doesn't always make sense.

Solomon deals with five areas of life that every person wonders about.

Inequity

Furthermore, I have seen under the sun that in the place of justice there is wickedness, and in the place of righteousness there is wickedness. (v. 16)

Solomon observes the inequity of life. Sometimes bad guys win and good guys suffer. Johnny Christian doesn't always score the touchdown, and Paul Pagan doesn't always fumble the ball. That's a fact.

Do you have a problem with that? Would you rather have a "perfect" universe?

Wouldn't it be great if, after a driver ran you off the road, his car would break down five minutes later? Or if someone cheated you in business, he would go bankrupt the next month? Or if someone got angry and yelled at you, her teeth would fall out that night? Wouldn't that be wonderful?

But unfortunately you'd have to live in the same universe. So if you gossiped about someone, your tongue would turn green. Every time you lusted or envied another person, more of your hair would fall out. Every time you spent money on something you didn't need, the food in your refrigerator would rot overnight.

Would you want to live in a world like that?

None of us want that kind of instant justice from God. God's patience with sin is an incredible blessing—otherwise, all of us would come under His immediate judgment.

I said to myself, "God will judge both the righteous man and the wicked man," for a time for every matter and for every deed is there. (v. 17)

Here's a fact to comfort us: There will be a day when God will deal with evil. The question is not, Why does God not punish evil? but, Why does He not punish evil now? He will deal with it. A guy once told me in a gym, "You know, good guys finish last." And I smiled and said, "Yeah, but bad guys go to hell." It will be one of the last chapters written.

> *I said to myself concerning the sons of men, "God has surely tested them in order for them to see that they are but beasts." For the fate of the sons of men and the fate of beasts is the same. As one dies so dies the other; indeed, they all have the same breath and there is no advantage for man over beast, for all is vanity. All go to the same place. All came from the dust and all return to the dust. (vv. 18–20)*

God tests man and shows him his fallibility. Under the sun, we are no different from the beasts. There is a greater difference between God and you than between you and the dust mites living on your skin. God tests us so that we recognize our great need and quickly repent. Death unveils the true human condition.

In contrast, verse 21 shows us that, unlike the beasts, man will have to face God one day.

> *Who knows that the breath of man ascends upward and the breath of the beast descends downward to the earth?*

Without revelation from God, man sees himself as just another animal. This is why man is losing his unique status in our secular culture today. Many people today are elevating animals to the status of humans. At the same time, others are dehumanizing people, especially the unborn, to the status of animals.

This is a humiliating thing. But in nature, both animals and people die. Solomon says that the difference is that people will face judgment by God.

So what should you do?

And I have seen that nothing is better than that man should be happy in his activities, for that is his lot. For who will bring him to see what will occur after him? (v. 22)

Solomon reiterates his earlier point: Do not let what you can't understand destroy what you can enjoy. As encouraged in the previous chapter, go eat some Rocky Road, find some good friends, and read a good book. Go catch a baseball game. Choose a beautiful afternoon, grab your friends and go sit in the stands, get a cold drink and a Snickers, and enjoy the game because we're all going to die someday.

Do you know what the word "lot" means in verse 22? It means a heritage—an inheritance. God gives you fun times right now. God gives you Rocky Road—that's the Hebrew. Don't live in constant fear of what might happen.

I have a friend whose father worked all of his life to retire at age fifty-five. He worked like a dog, denying himself all sorts of pleasure so he could retire before he was sixty. He finally made it.

At his retirement party, everybody celebrated and ate Italian food. At the end he stood up and said, "Thank you. Thank you. Thank you." Then he suddenly got woozy and passed out. His fainting was due to a brain tumor. Within six months, he was dead.

Enjoy right now. If you can change the bad stuff, change it. But if you can't, you better just enjoy life as it comes.

Oppression

In chapter 4 Solomon goes on to deal with the oppression and suffering he saw around him.

> *Then I looked again at all the acts of oppression*
> *which were being done under the sun. And behold I*
> *saw the tears of the oppressed and that they had no*
> *one to comfort them; and on the side of their oppres-*
> *sors was power, but they had no one to comfort them.*
> *(v. 1)*

I don't like that the bad guys hurt the good guys. I think we should work as hard as we can for justice. But the reality is that we still have men like Stalin and Hitler, and we've got genocide going on in a half a dozen countries right now. And it's going to keep happening as long as we are alive on this earth. The oppressors have the power, and the poor have no one to comfort them.

How can this be true? How does this evil occur just after Solomon has emphasized the sovereignty of God? It seems insane. Under the sun, you'd be better off dead.

> *So I congratulated the dead who are already dead*
> *more than the living who are still living. But better off*
> *than both of them is the one who has never existed,*
> *who has never seen the evil activity that is done under*
> *the sun. (vv. 2–3)*

Solomon laments that if you're alive, you can be sure somebody is going to hurt you unjustly. Oppression and injustice are a part of life.

Rivalry

Not only do we have to deal with oppression, Solomon says we also have to deal with rivalry.

And I have seen that every labor and every skill which is done is the result of rivalry between a man and his neighbor. This too is vanity and striving after wind. (v. 4)

Do you ever get tired of running in the rat race where only the rats win? Do you ever get weary of keeping up with the proverbial Joneses?

My generation got sick of the affluence of the 1950s. In the 1960s we bailed out and claimed the title of "flower children." Everybody just gave up ambition and the drive for financial success. We let our hair grow long, quit bathing, and just sat on the grass and hummed.

Solomon sounds like the first flower child. Why should we do something just to satisfy or impress somebody else? Some people never enjoy life because they're always trying to keep up a front. But Solomon shows us that we can take our denial of status quo too far.

The fool folds his hands and consumes his own flesh. One hand full of rest is better than two fists full of labor and striving after wind. (vv. 5–6)

If you quit working simply because of all the competition, you'll end up destroying yourself. In our modern culture, you have to work. You have to buy normal clothes that normal people wear. Dropping out is not an option for someone who wants to honor God.

But he also says that it doesn't make any sense to kill your-self to be a success in this world. Let me give you verse 6 in the Tommy Nelson Translation. Rather than putting two hands in for eighty hours a week, why don't you put in forty hours with one hand and with the other eat some Rocky Road?

All of those fancy clothes may look silly on you when you're eighty. And as for your flashy convertible, after you get about fifty-five years old, you won't be able to drive it anymore because you may feel like a fool. So Solomon says enjoy life with balance; don't focus solely on achievement and success.

Things over People

Then I looked again at vanity under the sun. There was a certain man without a dependent, having neither a son nor a brother, yet there was no end to all his labor. Indeed, his eyes were not satisfied with riches and he never asked, "And for whom am I laboring and depriving myself of pleasure?" This too is vanity and it is a grievous task. (vv. 7–8)

The word "dependent" in verse 8 means a partner. This "certain man" doesn't have a buddy to share his life with. Here's a guy who is working so hard but doesn't have any rela-tionships.

This is Ebenezer Scrooge. He works and works, comes home to a drafty house, counts his money, then goes to bed. And no one likes him. Solomon is giving us a picture of Scrooge.

This guy has no friend, no son, no brother, no family—nobody that he loves. But there's still no end to his labor. His eyes are not satisfied with riches, and he never asks the ques-tion, Why am I depriving myself of pleasure?

What's the evil we're looking at in verse 8? It's accumulating wealth at the expense of relationships. It's focusing more on things than on people.

How many mothers and fathers have shortchanged their children for $10,000 or $20,000 extra a year? How many young consultants make great money but don't have any friends because they travel every week? How many "Scrooges" have accumulated huge nest eggs but no friends?

Ty Cobb, the great Detroit Tiger whose harsh demeanor continuously alienated others, said, "If I had it to do over, I'd make more friends."

Solomon gives us advice on the value of relationships.

Two are better than one because they have a good return for their labor. For if either of them falls, the one will lift up his companion. But woe to the one who falls when there is not another to lift him up. Furthermore, if two lie down together they keep warm, but how can one be warm alone? And if one can overpower him who is alone, two can resist him. A cord of three strands is not quickly torn apart. (vv. 9–12)

Solomon reminds us that life is met by two people better than by one. Working together, two people can be more productive than one. If it gets cold, they can also keep each other warm. They can protect each other when danger comes. And if two is good, then three good friends are even stronger together.

The idea is that we shouldn't make money then stay away from people so we can keep more money. If we do that, we've forgotten life. Life is buddies. Life is pals. Life is partners and friends.

Even though I enjoy my wife tremendously, there are times when I need to get with a hairy-legged guy. I'll grab a good bud and say, "Let's go to Outback and just eat, talk, and tell stories about how great we were in high school."

Solomon asks, "What's the use of accumulating all this money if you don't have any friends?" This is one of the secrets to navigating life.

Are you lonely? Don't be lonely for the wrong reason: Don't be lonely by design. Be a loving, giving, kind, servant-hearted friend. Life is cold when you're by yourself. In this world, we all need a little help from our friends.

Someone told me to make sure every day to study and minister and play. Even though I got in the ministry to teach the Word, I need to make sure that I enjoy life with people. And so do you.

Life is not just making a living or performing a function. It is experiencing the delight of people. Cultivate and protect your friends. Develop friendships with willful acts of enjoyment. Protect your friends by constant acts of courtesy and sensitivity. Make sure that you stay in touch with people.

When it's all said and done, the only thing you'll have with you at your funeral will be your friends and family. The people who made money from your work won't be there, but your friends will. And they will be crying.

Popularity

In verse 13, Solomon looks at popularity.

A poor, yet wise lad is better than an old and foolish king who no longer knows how to receive instruction. For he has come out of prison to become king, even though he was born poor in his kingdom. I have

seen all the living under the sun throng to the side of
the second lad who replaces him. There is no end to
all the people, to all who were before them, and even
the ones who will come later will not be happy with
him, for this too is vanity and striving after wind.
(vv. 13–16)

Solomon sees that many people are hoping to be popular and famous. As a matter of fact, these verses hit close to home for him because they evoke the memory of his father, King David.

Even though David was born poor in his kingdom, under God's hand, David rose to become the ruler of Israel. Then the son took over, and Solomon says the whole world came out to celebrate the young guy. Isn't popularity wonderful?

But look at verse 16: There is no end to the people who will not be happy with you.

How quickly, Solomon says, they will forget you. Don Meredith used to say about quarterbacks, "Today you're in the penthouse. Tomorrow you're in the outhouse."

If you want to be a famous actress, have a great time. But don't make a bad movie because the press will absolutely dog you. No matter how naturally pretty you are, don't gain ten pounds because an editor will stick your "fat" face on the front of a magazine, and everybody in the grocery store checkout line will laugh at you. Do you like to wear nice clothes? Don't experiment with rowdy styles or you'll get stuck on the worst-dressed list, and then Letterman and Leno will make fun of you for a month.

Try this on your own? Become president of the Rotary Club. Get elected chairman of your Homeowners Association. You'll be doing great if more than half the people still like you when you're done.

Do you really want to get on that slippery slope of popularity by seeking the approval of men? Isn't it great to be normal with no one caring about what we think because we're just average people? There is a blessedness to anonymity sometimes.

Instead, Solomon says, trust God, do good, let the chips fall where they may, and enjoy life. Find some buddies, make all the money you can in a hard day's work, then go home and sit loose.

Do some things that will matter for eternity. Serve Christ as long as you can until your number comes up, then die well. Enjoy the things you do know and don't be so concerned and distraught about things you don't.

That's pretty good stuff for a three-thousand-year-old book. It's sound wisdom, and only a fool would ignore it to his peril.

But sometimes it is easier said than done, particularly when we see the wicked prosper and the righteous suffer. That's why in the next chapter we'll discuss Solomon's advice about dealing with the tough times we face.

For Discussion and Application

1. Have you known people who bailed out when something bad happened to them? Did they come back?

2. Do you have friends that will stick with you in tough times? What forces keep you from forming real relationships? How can you overcome them?

3. How do our expectations of God lead us to disappointment with Him? How do those expectations affect you?

4. What are some of the answers for dealing with the seeming insanity of life? How can you live sanely in an insane world?

CHAPTER 5

A Proper View
of Tough Times

ECCLESIASTES 5:1–6:12

How Should I Respond
When Wicked People Get Ahead in Life?

When I visit with people older than I am, I always ask them a question: "If you had to do life over, what would you do differently?" Most of the time they say something like, "I would not have overlooked so many 'todays' because of my ambitions for tomorrow. I wish I had smelled the roses more. I wish I hadn't worried so much because now I'm so old I can't even remember all the things I was worried about."

I get similar answers because all of us sometimes put our hope in something that might happen in the future. We become the proverbial donkey always reaching for the carrot. We're on a carousel, trying to catch the brass ring.

An Outline of Ecclesiastes
Following the Logic of Solomon
IV. Be Cautious About Impertinence Toward God: 5:1–7
    Be careful how you approach, speak to, and "bargain with" our mysterious God.
V. Be Correct in Perspective: 5:8–7:29
    Wealth: Don't be deceived when the wicked increase; wealth won't satisfy (5:8–6:12).

71

There are two ways to learn something in life. The first way you can learn things is in retrospect or with hindsight. That's where life gives you a whipping and you learn a lesson.

Now this way to learn is no fun. The tuition is high and the assignments are painful. A lot of times you can't repeat the class and are left with scars that won't go away.

The other way to learn is by wisdom. That's where you get a mentor who is smarter than you and listen to him. One of the marvelous things about the Word of God is that it is a treasure of timeless wisdom: "By them [God's judgments] Thy servant is warned; / In keeping them there is great reward" (Ps. 19:11).

In chapter 5 of Ecclesiastes, Solomon gives a caution and also some comfort. He shows us that there are some very good, logical, reasonable answers to deal with theodicy (the problem of evil existing under God's rule).

You may not think that this section is the most practical part of Ecclesiastes at first, but I can guarantee that you will apply this to your life. Sooner or later you are going to see oppression and wickedness succeed. That's when you'll remember these verses and the wisdom of Solomon.

One thing Solomon reminds us of is that evil won't ultimately be victorious. Even though God's plan may include Joseph going into the pit, then into Potiphar's house, then into prison; nevertheless, the last chapter will always vindicate Him. God causes all things to work together for good. He's still in charge.

So how should we react to the injustice and inequity around us? Solomon warns us about becoming bitter, angry, and withdrawn. He's going to tell us that we can't just check out because our little God didn't behave.

So God didn't jump through the hoops like you wanted Him to. Don't become aloof. Don't become unfaithful and hopeless.

Do you know of people who walk with God, living a

hunky-dory life until a family member or friend dies or hurts them and they find out that there are hypocrites among Christians? When life doesn't work out just the way they want, they bail. Do you know anybody like that?

Attitude

In Ecclesiastes Solomon tells us we need to be careful about our attitudes when we come to God.

> *Guard your steps as you go to the house of God, and draw near to listen rather than to offer the sacrifice of fools; for they do not know they are doing evil. (5:1)*

Guard your heart toward God. God does not delight in a fool. Why? Because a fool unknowingly does evil by challenging God. After all, we're only here for eighty years or so and can't even scratch places on our own backs unless we have someone to help us. We couldn't write our names in cursive until we were eight. Who are we to lift our heads against the infinite, immutable Almighty?

Solomon says we have to watch how we approach God, being careful in how we speak to Him.

> *Do not be hasty in word or impulsive in thought to bring up a matter in the presence of God. For God is in heaven and you are on the earth; therefore let your words be few. (v. 2)*

Did your mother ever say, "Watch your tone of voice?" My mother used to say that all the time: "Young man, do you want to change that tone of voice?" Then she'd give me some incentive to change—right on my bottom.

Solomon reminds us of the vast difference between God and humans. He is holy, invisible, and exalted, and you are on earth. God does not have a problem; you have the problem.

It's popular in some circles to vent at God, and while it is honest and appropriate to come to God in our desperation, take a lesson from God's warning to Job: it can be impious to do so.

Do you know what He said to Job? He didn't give Job any answers but asked him seventy questions, including, "Where were you when I laid the foundation of the earth? Do you know where the rain comes from, and do you know where the deer calve? Do you know why an ostrich lays eggs and gives up her babies and doesn't look after them?" God says, "I know the answer to these questions, do you?" He shows Job how foolish it is for him to try to tell Him how to run the universe.

Remember how Job's buddies came along and said, "Obviously you've done evil because only good things happen to good people"? What did God do at the end of the book? He made Job's buddies offer a sacrifice for their wicked counsel.

Since we can't see or understand everything, we should be careful about what we say to God.

Do you know why? Look at verse 3—this is brilliant.

For the dream comes through much effort, and the voice of a fool through many words.

Just as hard work produces sleep, so a fool produces many words and much pontificating. In contrast, Solomon says that men of effort are known for their dreams. They work hard and they are *silent*.

Can you say to God that you are mixed-up and need some answers? Certainly. God wants us to be honest with Him. But He also wants us to be careful how we approach Him. You have to watch your tone of voice. We may ask why but not with anger or impertinence. There can be no accusations as though God were not in control, nor bitterness as though we sit in judgment over Him.

Solomon also recognizes that sometimes we want to bargain with God.

> When you make a vow to God, do not be late in paying it, for He takes no delight in fools. Pay what you vow! It is better that you should not vow than that you should vow and not pay. Do not let your speech cause you to sin and do not say in the presence of the messenger of God that it was a mistake. Why should God be angry on account of your voice and destroy the work of your hands? (vv. 4–6)

In the heathen cultures of Solomon's time, people kept idols in their homes. They kept them nearby because if they placated the deities of the rain, the sun, the moon, and fertility, then they would have the gods working their side of the street.

But that tactic is an abomination to God. Don't make vows to try to manipulate God. Don't read your Bible as if it were a divine rabbit's foot. God wants us to pray and ask Him to change things, but He does not delight in scheming fools. Don't make God angry by toying with Him.

Verse 7 is phenomenal.

> For in many dreams and in many words there is emptiness. Rather, fear God.

The reference to many dreams goes back to verse 3. The dream comes through much effort. Men fall asleep because they work so hard. But "in many dreams . . . there is emptiness." Though the hard worker falls asleep at nine o'clock, he will still find nothing but emptiness.

The reference to many words also goes back to verse 3—the anger of a fool against God who speaks out angrily in many words. Whether it's a workaholic or an angry person who cries out against God, both shall find emptiness. "Rather, fear God."

I worked with a woman once who was agoraphobic—afraid of public places. People with this fear cannot deal with life and choose to stay in the safety of their homes.

This woman has wasted most of her life just sitting in her house. She is a beautiful, intelligent, gifted, loving woman, but she couldn't get over her bitterness toward a God who wouldn't fit into her box because He allowed evil to befall her. She never recovered from that bad experience and eventually imprisoned herself in her home.

In my church college group was a girl who was beaten by her father. She has never gotten past the abuse. It poisoned her and turned her into a great, big twenty-two-year-old boil. Every time people would get near her, all they would find was venom.

She is a beautiful young woman, but she has alienated every male and female within a thirty-mile radius. She is still miserable simply because she will not trust God with what she can't understand.

The reality is that anyone who wastes a lifetime accusing and questioning God is a fool. These women's dreams and words call God to the bar of human reason. They do not fear Him; on the contrary, they believe that because their lives aren't perfect, God is somehow wrong. But someone who continually whines about life is morally at odds with God.

In many words, just as in many dreams, there is emptiness.

Whether you're a believer or an atheist, you will royally mess up your life if you can't trust God.

In the next section Solomon deals with the frustration we feel when we see wicked people succeeding and accruing wealth.

If you see oppression of the poor and denial of justice and righteousness in the province, do not be shocked at the sight, for one official watches over another official, and there are higher officials over them. (v. 8)

Don't be shocked and surprised. Don't throw your hands in the air and say, "Alas, there is no God." Don't get too upset because what goes around will come around. Ultimately, evil men will be caught because God is the final tribunal.

Psalm 73:18 says that God sets the wicked in "slippery places." They are confident now, but somebody will deal with them eventually.

Ecclesiastes 5:9 is the most textually problematic verse in the book. About twenty different possible interpretations can be made as to how the Hebrew actually reads.

The New American Standard says,

After all, a king who cultivates the field is an advantage to the land.

But the New King James Version says, "Moreover the profit of the land is for all; even the king is served from the field."

So which does it mean? I'll give you what I think is the best solution. Verse 8 alludes to evil men having to answer to a higher power—eventually, God. They're not sovereign. They're not free. Somebody will deal with them.

It appears that verse 9 in the King James Version substanti-
ates the idea of the comeuppance for evil men in verse 8. The
blessing of the Lord is for all. Even a king needs the blessing of
God upon the field. A king is not sovereign. He looks to God to
bless the land. These wicked men must deal with those above
them who must deal ultimately with a sovereign God.

Solomon goes on to talk about the wealth that evil men
accrue.

The Problem with Wealth

*He who loves money will not be satisfied with money,
nor he who loves abundance with its income. This too
is vanity. When good things increase, those who consume them increase. So what is the advantage to their
owners except to look on? The sleep of the working
man is pleasant, whether he eats little or much. But
the full stomach of the rich man does not allow him to
sleep. (vv. 10–12)*

The man who loves money is in a Catch-22—he wants
something that will never satisfy him. Desire always outruns
possessions. No one ever reaches that certain amount when he
says, "I make $100,000 and I don't want to make a cent more."
No one goes to his boss and says, "Please, no more raises. I'm
making all I'll ever need."

Once you've had it, Solomon says, you'll want more of it.
This desire is like a fire that keeps burning and consuming. So
don't be fooled.

Not only does wealth not satisfy but it also complicates
your life. And even if wealth doesn't change you, it will change
everyone around you. Did you ever notice that when a heavy-
weight fighter climbs into the ring, a pack of people climb in

the ring with him? Usually about four or five people follow and hover around him like snowy egrets picking the ticks off a cow.

That's what money does. Proverb 14:20 says, "Those who love the rich are many." Everybody's your buddy. Why do you think some rich guys go buy a thousand acres in Wyoming? It's to get away from people because they don't know whom to trust anymore.

When you don't have any money, if someone likes you, it's just for who you are. Aren't you glad? Cornelius Vanderbilt said, "A million dollars is more than any mortal should have to bear." Of course, a million dollars was a lot of money in his day, but the point is, when you have money, everybody will want a piece of you.

So don't marvel when wicked people accrue wealth. In the end they won't get away with it. They are never satisfied and their lives become very complicated.

Solomon says that wealth also distracts you. An hourly worker doesn't have enough money to get himself in a lot of trouble. He works hard and gets tired. At the end of the day, he comes home, eats, watches the tube a little while, then goes to bed and sleeps well.

But that's not how it is for the rich man. He has to worry about how his money is being spent. If he doesn't keep making money, they will come and take away his playthings.

No one wants to make $1,000,000 so that he can spend $20,000 a year and save the other $980,000. People who make $1,000,000 spend it on the things that other millionaires spend it on. They always worry because they have to make sure the stocks don't crash or that someone somewhere doesn't make a decision that sets off a chain reaction of events that can sink them. Wealth generally does not give rest.

One of the Hunt brothers was asked, "Is it true that you make a million dollars a day?" He said, "Son, I would starve on a million dollars a day." Can you imagine?

Wealth Weakens You

Not only does wealth complicate your life, it can also weaken you.

There is a grievous evil which I have seen under the sun: riches being hoarded by their owner to his hurt.
(v. 13)

If you have wealth and don't know how to use it, it can hurt you. I saw a documentary recently about the Temptations. They were high school kids having fun singing on the corner, then somebody heard them, and suddenly they were Motown. They got famous. And you know what? Today only one of those guys is still alive.

One shot himself because of his alcoholism and a broken marriage—both of which were caused by wealth.

Another used his money to get into drugs. He was found with a bullet through his head after he had been thrown out of a drug pusher's limousine.

Another one of them committed adultery and destroyed his marriage.

Life was simple until they got money. They didn't know how to deal with it and became real-life examples of wealth accumulated by man to his hurt.

Have you ever considered that one of God's great mercies toward you is that He restricts the amount of money you make?

Solomon then gives us an illustration.

When those riches were lost through a bad investment and he had fathered a son, then there was nothing to support him. As he had come naked from his mother's womb, so will he return as he came. He will take nothing from the fruit of his labor that he can carry in his hand. (vv. 14–15)

It's as if the money that the owner made ends up mocking him. He lost the money that he depended on, and now he has a son to support.

He also had to face his own mortality. How much will a rich man leave? Everything. Every single dime. The only time in the Bible that God personally calls a man a fool is in Luke 12:19–20: "And I [a rich man] will say to my soul, 'Soul, you have many goods laid up for many years to come; take your ease, eat, drink and be merry.' But God said to him, 'You fool! This very night your soul is required of you; and now who will own what you have prepared?'"

The rich man loses everything he had put his faith in. Store up treasures in heaven, not here, because wealth in the hands of a man who doesn't know how to use it is a severe affliction.

If you're a person who lives for accruing wealth—thinking that it will give you status, significance, and happiness—it will actually be a blessing if God halts your progress. Otherwise, at the end of your life, you would have to hear the soft laughter of your money as you leave everything behind.

And this also is a grievous evil—exactly as a man is born, thus he will die. So, what is the advantage to him who toils for the wind? Throughout his life he also eats in darkness with great vexation, sickness and anger. (vv. 16–17)

Thus Solomon asks the question in Ecclesiastes 5:16, "What's it all for?" All accomplishments are sand castles. Tomorrow will wash them away. And not only will they elude you in eternity, but verse 17 says they can remove the joy of today. The pressure of wealth produces worry, sickness, and anger. The daydream of wealthy men is quite often earlier days of simplicity where things were less complex and worrisome.

How We Should Use Wealth

Here is what I have seen to be good and fitting: to eat, to drink and enjoy oneself in all one's labor in which he toils under the sun during the few years of his life which God has given him; for this is his reward. Furthermore, as for every man to whom God has given riches and wealth, He has also empowered him to eat from them and to receive his reward and rejoice in his labor; this is the gift of God. For he will not often consider the years of his life, because God keeps him occupied with the gladness of his heart. (vv. 18–20)

Solomon says that we shouldn't see wealth as the goal of our lives; rather, we should see wealth as a means to do good and bring enjoyment. Don't try to collect it and show it off to everybody. Instead, savor life's Rocky Road. Catch some baseball games. Enjoy your money. A wise person is too busy enjoying today to worry about every little detail concerning the future.

God provides people with the ability to make wealth. But God is also the only one who can provide the ability to enjoy wealth and see it for what it is.

Every time we have made more money, my wife and I have made sure to do a couple of things. I believe these are an application of Solomon's wisdom.

First, always take a portion off the top of your income and give it to the Lord's work. Then hold the rest of your funds with a loose hand and use them for good. Give money away. Use it to help people. Also, use some of it for pure enjoyment—to go someplace or see something.

My wife and I have decided that at the end of our lives, we don't want to have just a big closet of clothes that no longer fit us. We want to be able to enjoy what we have now.

Are you enjoying life right now? Are you celebrating the blessing of God in your life materially? In John 10:10 Jesus says, "I came that they might have life, and might have it abundantly."

You can have an abundant life whether you have a little money or a lot. Don't think that you have to skip over today to get to tomorrow's utopia. That's vanity. Enjoy what God gives.

In chapter 5 of Ecclesiastes, Solomon has shown us the importance of correctly evaluating people and their lives. We tend to look at a wicked person who is beautiful, wealthy, or talented, and we immediately think that's unfair.

But in chapter 6, Solomon shows us that prosperity is not always good. In chapter 7, he will tell us that affliction is not always the worse thing. "Those whom the Lord loves He disciplines" (Heb. 12:6). He flunks us and makes us repeat a grade again.

The chances are that if I asked you to list the things that have shaped your life, you would not name the mountaintop moments of success. Instead, you would list your times in valleys of hurt and pain when you were forced to rely on trust, prayer, and perseverance. Those are the times that shape you.

Imagine you had a child to whom you gave everything she wanted all the time. If she never had to struggle for anything, how do you think that child would turn out?

The Bible says discipline your child while there is hope. Don't let your child have everything. Proverbs 20:21 says, "An inheritance gained hurriedly at the beginning, / Will not be blessed in the end." Too much good is often a bad thing.

It doesn't make any sense to give all the things you worked so hard for to your children without any effort on their part. That is how you spoil children—by giving your high-priced goods to your kids for free.

Why would parents do that? Because they're foolish and think the best thing that can ever happen to someone is the absence of pain and the presence of pleasure. Do you believe that?

I don't know about you, but I had patriotic parents. My dad would lay stripes on me and I would see stars. If you do a survey of successful, balanced adults, I'll guarantee a high percentage of them had patriotic parents too.

I'm not talking about being abusive, but we need parents who won't tolerate sloth, foolishness, and evil. They need to be willing to give momentary pain so that their children won't experience ultimate disaster. My dad did this for me and I cried then, but now (hopefully) I won't be crying when I am sixty because I'm still a fool.

We need parents to love their children enough to challenge them. We have to set boundaries and let our children butt up against them.

God is a parent like this. He loves you enough not to tolerate junk in your life. The modern "prosperity gospel" that says prosperity is always best and hardship is always bad is just plain wrong. Solomon doesn't buy it.

Some of us may be stuck in the mind-set of "since bad things are happening to me, God doesn't love me." Solomon challenges this idea by saying that bad things sometimes are really for your good.

Let me give you an illustration. I just read the book *The Greatest Generation*. When I started reading it, I said, "Hallelujah, somebody's finally written this book." I'm almost fifty, and I've been watching the generation before me for years. They were boys and girls in the depression, raised by parents who went through World War I. Then when those kids went through World War II, they already knew how to sacrifice. They were willing to sacrifice their lives and their children. They learned how to pray because they knew the most evil man of our century was running amuck.

These depression kids who went through World War II were shaped by struggle, heartache, and poverty. They were the backbone that preserved America and kept democracy alive in the world.

This generation went through an incredible amount of pain. And what was the result? They ended up (for the most part) God-fearing, economical, persevering, prayerful, courageous, tough, and strong. They're the greatest generation this country has ever produced.

Do you know why? Because of the pain, poverty, disaster, war, death, blood, tears, and all that stuff they endured.

But a lot of them made a mistake with us—their children— bless their hearts. They said, "I want to make sure my child never goes through what I went through." So the country produced a generation that skipped the same struggles. Look at the baby boomers today; they're a mess. Now we've had several generations that know nothing but three square meals, multiple televisions, and a car at sixteen. So many young people are flashy, plump, illusory voyeurs with no real "core." Thank you, prosperity!

If you've been going through hard times, I hope you'll stop right here, face God, and ask Him to use this suffering to make you into something. His adversity is like a chisel and hammer in your life. To paraphrase C. S. Lewis, "Maybe God will teach you to get rid of all your toys and grow up."

Wealth without Wisdom

Solomon challenges our assumptions in chapter 6. Here he describes a man with wealth but no capacity to enjoy it.

> *There is an evil which I have seen under the sun and it is prevalent among men—a man to whom God has given riches and wealth and honor so that his soul lacks nothing of all that he desires, but God has not empowered him to eat from them, for a foreigner enjoys them. This is vanity and a severe affliction. (vv. 1–2)*

Most of us think it would be great to have wealth and honor. But here those acquisitions are an evil because the man can't enjoy what he has. This man has success, but he doesn't know the God who gave it and so he can't appreciate it.

This is a painful thing to see and an even more painful thing to experience.

> *If a man fathers a hundred children and lives many years, however many they be, but his soul is not satisfied with good things, and he does not even have a proper burial, then I say, "Better the miscarriage than he, for it comes in futility and goes into obscurity; and*

its name is covered in obscurity. It never sees the sun
and it never knows anything; it is better off than he.
Even if the other man lives a thousand years twice and
does not enjoy good things—do not all go to one
place?" (vv. 3–6)

Now this is incredible. Here is a man who lives many years
and has one hundred children. But he doesn't know how to
enjoy what he has because he doesn't recognize it is from God.
Solomon says it would be better for that man if he had never
lived.

The oldest man in the Old Testament lived for about 960
years; nobody made it to a thousand. Solomon's example is of
a two-thousand-year-old man. But if he doesn't enjoy the good
things of his life, every one of those years was a waste.

Someone like this is better off never being born because his
life is only vanity and a severe evil. Why? Because success can
never truly satisfy.

All a man's labor is for his mouth and yet the appetite
is not satisfied. For what advantage does the wise man
have over the fool? What advantage does the poor
man have, knowing how to walk before the living?
What the eyes see is better than what the soul desires.
This too is futility and a striving after wind. (vv. 7–9)

A man works and works to buy food, but it's never enough.
He has to keep working because he continually gets hungry and
needs to eat. Wealth will never sate you. It will never scratch
your itch deep enough.

I know a man who doesn't make much money but leases a
Lexus for his business. Now, you can be sure he doesn't tell

clients, "Climb into my leased Lexus." He makes them think it's his because he wants to create the illusion of being a big success. You can have a fake Rolex or a rented Lexus, but your appetite for more of these illusions will only grow.

You're never going to be ultimately happy in this life. So it's better to enjoy what you have than dream about what you don't.

Solomon says that the things your eyes see today are better than the things your soul would like to get tomorrow. Live today! Enjoy your friends. When you get off from work, leave it behind. Get with your buddies.

Does this sound familiar? Solomon repeats himself because he really wants us to understand this point.

If you're a single person, call your friends and go get a pizza. Catch a plane to see an old friend for the weekend. Go to the library and get that book you've wanted to read, then stop on the way home and get a cup of good, strong coffee.

Enjoy life now. Every morning my schedule is booked from 6:00 A.M. to 8:30 A.M. But at 8:30 I go down to the gym and hang out with a bunch of guys. We lift weights and lie about how great we used to be. These guys aren't Christians, but I love being with them, getting to share life with them, and eventually telling them about Christ.

I'm not going to sit around and look at my house and wonder how much better life could be if I had a bigger home. If you want a bigger house and can afford it, and you have your financial priorities in the correct place, build a bigger house. But don't think that a bigger house will ultimately make your life complete.

Solomon had more money than you can even comprehend and said wealth is not worth anything if you can't take a drive in the country, enjoy a piece of cheesecake, or watch a baseball game on a cool autumn night.

Solomon says we should celebrate and enjoy life for what it is—a precious gift from God.

Whatever exists has already been named, and it is known what man is; for he cannot dispute with him who is stronger than he is. (v. 10)

God created man and named him—He knows everything about man. He created Adam and Eve to enjoy each other. They were supposed to cultivate the garden and make something with their hands. We're told the trees in the garden were good for food and a delight to the eyes. See? That's proof positive that God made us to enjoy Him and to enjoy life.

Again, He made life to be enjoyed, not to be collected. God will not let us be happy through things. And we can't change that fact with Him, because He is stronger and wiser than we are. We can fight and stomp, but it won't make any difference.

For there are many words which increase futility. What then is the advantage to a man? (v. 11)

Solomon is basically saying that we can talk back to God all we want, but we will just end up frustrated. God says it will give you no advantage to argue. God has stacked the deck of life and is the dealer. He owns the casino. He has determined that "life is to know Me."

You may be going through some rough times right now and may not like what you are reading in this book. You don't want to trust God with your life. You don't want to have faith; you want explanations.

In this verse God says, "Tough." We can't return to Eden. Our only hope is to trust and enjoy Him. You can philosophize and rationalize until you are blue in the face, but God isn't going to change for you.

> *For who knows what is good for a man during his lifetime, during the few years of his futile life? He will spend them like a shadow. For who can tell a man what will be after him under the sun? (v. 12)*

Are we smart enough to even understand Him if He told us? You and I, who don't know how to program a VCR? You and I, who can't remember what we had for breakfast two weeks ago?

Solomon says we spend our lives like a shadow. The sun comes up and creates a shadow, then the sun goes down and the shadow is gone. Compared to God's existence, our lives are as momentary and fleeting as a shadow.

And when our lives are gone, we have no control over how we are remembered. We hope to leave something behind that will give us a lasting legacy. But Solomon says that there are no guarantees; it's all in God's hands.

Solomon is very dogmatic in this section because he wants to put us in our place. The only choice we have is to be miserable or happy. Many words and protests will simply end in frustration.

God says that He has made everything and knows what will ultimately make us happy. He tells us not to be so dumb as to think that happiness comes from toys. You won't be happy as long as you are deceived, thinking that the best thing for you is a perfect life. God says you are sorely mistaken.

In the next chapter, Solomon will show us that the worst thing in life is not affliction. God wants us to be happy, but He knows that true happiness comes only through walking with Him by faith no matter what life brings.

For Discussion and Application

1. What are some lessons you have learned that have had a "high tuition"? Are there things you did not learn except from experience? What was that process like?

2. What are some of the things you do just to enjoy life?

3. Tommy suggests that life is what it is, and our only choice is to be miserable or happy. Think back to times when you have made that choice. What factors influenced your attitude? How do we make the choice to be happy?

4. Tommy says, "Let God shape you through the chisel and hammer of adversity." How has God used hard times in your life to shape you and draw you closer to Him?

CHAPTER 6

When Bad
Is Better

ECCLESIASTES 7:1–14

How Should I Feel
about the Bad Times I Go Through?

If you ever listen to a tape from Denton Bible Church, you can be sure it was produced and mailed from the Allie Miller Memorial Tape Library. Allie was a businessman who established the church's tape library and developed its recording, storing and filing system and mailing protocols.

He was about sixty years old when he died from prostate cancer. Before he died, Allie told me that the greatest thing that ever happened to him—other than knowing Jesus Christ—was cancer. I asked him how this could possibly be true. He replied that cancer was the thing that finally put everything in perspective.

Allie came to know the Lord when he was a little boy. But, he said, "I used Him as my Savior." Allie was a wonderful

---

An Outline of Ecclesiastes
Following the Logic of Solomon
V. Be Correct in Perspective: 5:8–7:29
    Wealth: Don't be deceived when the wicked increase; wealth
      won't satisfy (5:8–6:12).
    Adversity: Hard times are not bad; they shape us (7:1–14).

fellow, but he never really committed his life to eternal things until God showed him that he was going to die. He said, "When you have a death pronouncement given to you, you don't have to take it by faith that you're going to die. Now all that stuff you've been saying all those years about laying up your treasures takes on real meaning."

Allie began to serve Christ because he knew every day was a tick of the clock. And from that appreciation and realization, he could say that the greatest thing that ever happened to him other than Jesus Christ was the appointment God gave him with cancer.

Trials always have a very beneficial purpose. Trials purify you. Trials show you what you are. Whatever comes out of you when you're hit, shows who you really are. When you're jostled, trials show that you can't make it on your own. Trials perfect you. Trials bring you to the end of your physical, intellectual rope. Trials make you pray. Trials make you go to the Word. Trials make you trust. Trials make everything you heard in Sunday school become real. Trials make you go to Christ.

Trials also prove you. Jesus says when persecution arises because of the Word, immediately those who are temporarily rooted in Christ fall away (Matt. 13:21). Peter says that the proof of your faith is "more precious than gold which is perishable, [and] even though tested by fire, may be found to result in praise and glory and honor at the revelation of Jesus Christ" (1 Pet. 1:7). Trials reveal who the real guys are.

Trials also humanize you. Trials make you sweet and sensitive. Paul Newman has a foundation for alcohol recovery. Do you know why? Because he lost a boy to alcohol. Carroll O'Connor has a foundation for drug rehab. Do you know why? Because he lost a boy to drugs. Liz Taylor spends a lot of time and money supporting AIDS research. Do you know why? Because she has lost so many friends in Hollywood to it. She was softened by the pain.

Have you seen the movie *The Doctor* with William Hurt? He was an arrogant surgeon until he got cancer and learned to be sensitive. *Regarding Henry* with Harrison Ford is about an arrogant lawyer who gets shot in the head and finds out he can be a very fallible, gentle, kind person. That's what trials do. They do good things in us. The only problem is that these trials are things we don't necessarily want to experience.

In chapter 7 of Ecclesiastes, Solomon says that hard times are not always the worst thing.

In the time of Solomon, people put on oil or ointments for a party, for happiness, for frivolity. When you were gearing up for your biggest party, you would break out the best ointment and go have a good time.

Our culture is similar to Solomon's. Most people go through life looking to have a good time. We dress up and go out to eat, visit friends, or catch a movie—essentially trying to have as much fun as we can.

That's why it's so crucial that we hear what Solomon is saying. God shows that He is not so committed to our short-term happiness as He is to our character. He tells us what really matters—and that's having a good name, not having a good "ointment" or good times.

> *A good name is better than a good ointment,*
> *And the day of one's death is better than the day of*
>   *one's birth. (v. 1)*

God says that He wants us to have a good name, meaning that He wants us to become men and women of nobility and righteousness. He doesn't want only to bless us; He wants to change us. He doesn't want our smiles and laughter; He wants our hearts. He wants us to grow up and resemble Christ.

So how does God bring this change about? How does He create holiness, character, and joy in us? Through pain and suffering.

If you want character and a good name, sometimes death is better than life. Sometimes a funeral is better than a party, because pain makes you real. Pain can get your thinking straight.

My son Benjamin is a free spirit. You've heard it said of certain kids that "they walk to their own drummer"? Ben had his own marching band.

Sometimes when children have a problem listening to their daddy, it's because they have a wax buildup. But if you heat their rear end up about 15 degrees, it will melt that wax.

Ben was having a problem hearing me, so I cleared the wax out of his ears. I said, "Benjamin, can you hear me now?" He said, "I hear *real* good."

The pain of discipline was part of how God wanted me to help shape the character of my son.

Solomon says God wants to give you a good name, not just a good time. Pain is an integral part of that process. Why? Because good times can fool you.

Good Times Are Deceitful

It is better to go to a house of mourning
Than to go to a house of feasting,
Because that is the end of every man,
And the living takes it to heart.
Sorrow is better than laughter,
For when a face is sad a heart may be happy. (vv. 2–3)

Plenty of people in America are having a good time, but they are deceived. They use pleasure to dull the pain so they don't have to acknowledge the deep needs of their souls.

Solomon says it's better to go to a funeral because in a house of mourning you see the end of every man. The wise man is smart enough to take it to heart. The house of mourning will change you.

I can go preach a sermon at a bar, but people don't want to listen because they're too busy laughing. But whenever I conduct a funeral, I have the audience's full attention. Every funeral is a reminder that one day you are going to die.

The wise person recognizes the benefit of pain—even pain like Allie Miller's when he heard the prognosis from his doctor. It sobers you; it makes you think long and hard.

I remember a man named Dave who had quite a few Christian friends who would tell him about how he could have a relationship with Christ, but he would never listen.

Dave was an outdoorsman and loved to go camping. One night he was camping in the woods during a storm, and as he lay in his sleeping bag, he was struck by lightning. It shook him up. Some of his friends told him he needed to get right with God. But he still didn't listen.

You know what they say about lightning never striking twice? Forget it! A couple of weeks later, Dave was out camping again and this time he really got zapped. The lightning welded the zipper on his sleeping bag. They had to cut him out of his cocoon. His friends again told him about the love of Christ, but he still didn't turn to God.

A few weeks later, Dave's neighbors were eating breakfast early one morning when they heard a loud boom and felt their whole house shake. They thought a truck had driven into the side of their house.

When they went outside, they saw smoke coming from Dave's house, then Dave coming out of his house. His hair was burnt and frizzy, and there were little ringlets of smoke coming from where his eyebrows used to be.

It turns out that he had a gas leak in his house. The gas turned his house into a bomb he'd set off when he flicked on some electricity. He had second-degree burns over much of his body. They rushed him into the shower and turned the cold water on his second-degree burns. The whole time Dave was shouting, "God's trying to tell me something! God's trying to tell me something!" They ended up leading him to Christ.

Why is sorrow better than laughter? Because, the text says, a person who is laughing is not really facing reality. He's not learning anything about the nature of life; he's just pretending that happiness will make him whole. But man's highest purpose is not simply to enjoy life, but rather to know God.

When a person's face is sad, his heart may end up happy because he's learned some things. Allie was sad at that doctor's report, but his heart was happy. Dave was sad when he was smoking in that shower, but his heart was happy because he'd found God.

Too often, we are not impressed by truth or doctrine, but we are always shaped by pain. Hard times can make you wise.

Hard Times Bring Wisdom

The mind of the wise is in the house of mourning,
While the mind of fools is in the house of pleasure.
It is better to listen to the rebuke of a wise man
Than for one to listen to the song of fools. (vv. 4–5)

The mind of the fool is at the disco. The mind of a fool is at the bar. The mind of a fool is at the house of feasting, the house of pleasure. The mind of a fool thinks the Christian life should be painless.

A friend told me a story that illustrates this Scripture. He was visiting a church member's relative suffering from cancer. It seemed quite clear from the diagnosis and discernment that this dear lady was not going to recover. So his time there was spent in prayer and simple efforts to bring comfort to her and her family.

As he left he was passed in the doorway by some members of the church the family was currently attending. As they came in, they sang and made statements proclaiming that healing was already complete—as if she would jump right out of bed cancer-free and start dancing.

Shortly after the funeral, my friend learned that the other church's leadership confronted the woman's family and blamed her death on a lack of faith. The surviving family was devastated.

The mentality that the Christian life is all prosperity and no suffering is unwise if not downright stupid. It's never wrong to pray for healing. It's wrong to believe it's always for the best.

Hard times can make you smart. Why do people ask, "What would you do if you knew you had only one more day to live?" Because you will focus on what is important in the face of death.

Has God done this with you? A. W. Tozer once said, "God cannot use a man until He has hurt him deeply." You and I are not changed by doctrine or by theological knowledge. We enjoy it but we're not impressed until we get hurt. God has to hurt us to make it real. Great men and great women are shaped by pain.

You've probably had someone you respect approach you and say, "We need to talk." Then he turns the chairs so that you face one another, sits down slowly, and takes a deep breath. Meanwhile, your heart is racing and you're thinking, "Oh no!" Then he drops the bomb on you about some blind spot or area of sin in your life.

Is that an enjoyable thing? Of course not! At the time, it's a horrible thing. It's like drinking half a bottle of milk of magnesia and knowing you're about to get purged of everything in you. The things within you that shouldn't be there are leaving in just a little bit. Isn't that pleasant?

Wouldn't you rather listen to some random guy sing in a piano bar? Then you wouldn't have to deal with it. Wouldn't that be better than having some wise man tell you of sin in your life and direct you to change? Nobody enjoys an experience like that.

But do we need somebody to do that? Yes, we do. Our lives can be just fine if we never hear the singing fool in the piano bar. But we won't ever be truly happy if we don't have some wise folks who'll come alongside us and give us a good rebuke. If we can't take that rebuke, we'll be failures.

For as the crackling of thorn bushes under a pot,
So is the laughter of the fool,
And this too is futility. (v. 6)

Have you ever burned thorns? Thorns are great to start a fire with because they burn bright and hot. But they also burn quickly and then they're gone. While they're burning, they crackle and pop like laughter.

Solomon says that a fool's laughter is like burning thorns. It sounds great and makes a lot of noise, but it's also gone in a flash. It reminds me of a lot of the actors and singers we enjoy. Bless their hearts, they are fools. They are fun to listen to for a few minutes but contribute nothing of lasting value to our lives.

So Solomon says that the laughter of fools is a very deceptive thing. Laughter can also be a very tempting thing. But God's purpose is not to foster idiocy.

For oppression makes a wise man mad,
And a bribe corrupts the heart. (v. 7)

The Hebrew word for "mad" means "crazy," not "angry." Oppression makes you nuts. Oppression (or power) and longing for wealth (resorting to bribes) can corrupt and destroy.

The problem with being surrounded by happy, godless people is that those people can tempt you to oppression, wickedness, and bribery. If a wise man is surrounded continually by people who savor power, oppression, dominance, and wealth, it can make him lose his mind. It can eventually corrupt his heart.

I have seen God-fearing men surround themselves with guys on a faster track. These God-fearing men turn from their wives and children and burn every bridge that is precious to them. They throw away everything good and launch themselves out into a vacuum of nothingness all because they were surrounded by the laughter of fools.

The end of a matter is better than its beginning;
Patience of spirit is better than haughtiness of spirit.
(v. 8)

I really like this verse's wisdom.

What is louder: the beginning of a matter or the end of it? The beginning always makes more noise. Weddings are big, boisterous, ostentatious affairs. "I will love you faithfully until the end of your life" is declared while the piped-in music swells to a crescendo. Oh, what a beautiful couple.

It's OK for them to get off to a loud, gushing start, but check back in sixty years after they've hurt each other and cried and raised kids and gained about thirty-five pounds each. I guarantee the end won't be as loud and ostentatious as the beginning, but it sure is a lot more important.

The end of a matter is better than the beginning because the beginning is all talk. I love weddings, but I love something else even more. I love to do a funeral for an eighty-six-year-old man when his wife of sixty-five years is sitting there on the front pew—faithful to him to the end. There's not a lot of fluff to it, but it's just glorious. They endured the hardship and pain, ignored the laughter of fools, and they finished well. That's character.

The beginning is just great words. Vows are good, but they are just intentions of what you think you will do. It's a whole lot better to actually make it.

One time, I ran the White Rock Marathon in Dallas. It was a marvelous feat.

Before the race, I was at the starting line with about five college guys who looked like athletes. But they also looked like they'd just been out late the night before when one of them said, "Hey, y'all, let's run a marathon."

They were standing at the starting line with these red and blue beanies on their heads. The beanies had springs on the top with little twirly rods on the end. The guys were making jokes as we started running. I listened to them and could tell they were clever guys.

After about seven or eight miles, we were still running together and these guys were still joking. After about fourteen miles, the conversation hit a lull. After seventeen miles, these guys were not speaking and started sinking back in the pack. I lost sight of them. After about twenty miles, I was depleted of everything in my body and the training took over. I had trained well and eaten well and had enough residual drive to get me through to the end.

I had paid a fee to suffer this torture, but I was getting a T-shirt for it. My goal was to finish the marathon without ever having to walk, and I did it. I was a happy man; I finished in three hours and fifty-eight minutes.

It was rough! I'll never forget that when I was finishing the last mile, the race officials had a bagpipe player playing "Amazing Grace." I was so tired when I heard the bagpipes that I thought I was hearing my own funeral music. But I finally finished, and my wife was there for me at the end. A few of my buddies had come to meet me, and we chatted for about twenty minutes. Then they took my picture, and I got my little certificate for finishing the marathon.

About forty-five minutes after I had finished, we walked to the car. I spied a lone college guy still racing. You should have seen him. One of his twirly rods was missing off his beanie. The other rod was resting quietly on his forehead. His right side wasn't working very well, and he was limping to the end, hoping to make it over the finish line.

If I'd have known this verse at the time I'd have aptly said, "The end of the matter is better than the beginning." You can have a lot of laughter at the beginning, but I'll take the end where there's pain, perseverance, stick-to-itiveness, courage, preparation, and discipline. So Solomon says he is impressed by the guy that makes it to the end.

In verse 9, Solomon gives us an application.

Do not be eager in your heart to be angry,
For anger resides in the bosom of fools.

Solomon says to not be eager to be angry. Angry at whom? In this context, he is warning us about becoming angry at God Almighty.

Everyone is tempted to get mad at God sometimes. Maybe God let your sister die, let your father leave your mother, let you develop MS. Maybe your mate left you or a girl broke your heart.

Being a pastor, I can give you plenty of stories about people mad at God because He didn't do right. They didn't know He wasn't concerned with their ointments but with their good names. So when the hard times came, they got mad and stuck out their lips at the Almighty. Solomon says they are fools.

When you are afflicted, don't start pouting and fussing. Don't start pointing a finger at God, because you don't know what He's doing. Happiness and laughter can fool you. They are very overrated benefits.

We also have to be careful not to gripe at God as to why He doesn't do "like He always did before."

Do not say, "Why is it that the former days were
    better than these?"
For it is not from wisdom that you ask about this.
    (v. 10)

Why isn't God doing now what He did six months ago or a year ago? Your life was going great until you hit some bumps. You were soaking in the rains, and now you're going through a drought.

You're just a spoiled child who wants to eat peppermints rather than collard greens for dinner. And I've acted the same way. I don't want what's best for me; I want what's pleasant.

My son had a successful college baseball career at the University of Kansas. When I prayed for him, what do you think I said? "Oh, God, give my son four hits. Lord, let him steal two bases, get his name in the paper, and have the pros sign him for lots of money." That's what I would pray.

One week he was the Big Twelve player of the week. He hit about .670 for seven games. He led his team in all but one category. He was on a roll.

Then he went into a slump and didn't get a hit for four games. His average dropped from .379 to .301. He didn't touch first base.

I was praying and crying out to God for "better treatment" for my son. But then He reminded me that He is more concerned with my son's life than with his press coverage.

In my head, I know that God gives my son what is best for him. But when my son was going through his slump, I wanted to say, "Why are the former days so much better than today?"

I don't like God's process of purifying me, and you don't like His purifying of you. Does anybody really like milk of magnesia? Would you order it at a restaurant?

But we shouldn't gripe because God is doing a great thing in our lives.

Wisdom along with an inheritance is good
And an advantage to those who see the sun. (v. 11)

It's one thing to have a good life handed down to you from your parents; it's even better to have wisdom. That's why God is letting you experience hard times—because He's trying to make something out of you.

Having money is fine. Finding pleasure in life is great. Being in a position of power is OK. But can you have all of those things and be a total, miserable failure in life? Yes.

What if your character is shaped by God? Then you are guaranteed a success that matters in the end. That's what He wants.

Wisdom Is Protection

For wisdom is protection just as money is protection. But the advantage of knowledge is that wisdom preserves the lives of its possessors. (v. 12)

Money can protect us from a lot of things in this world, but it can't protect us as well as wisdom. Solomon says that when God brings pain into our lives, He is often growing wisdom in us. And in the end, He is protecting us.

In my church is a nine-year-old boy named Mark. He is amazing to talk to. He is mature and gentle.

You've seen how nine-year-olds can treat someone who looks different or makes a mistake? They're like piranha—they consume them and strip their bones. Not Mark. He is full of love, tenderness, happiness, and sympathy. Do you know why?

Mark has a little brother named Timmy who has Down's syndrome. From the time Timmy was little, Mark learned how to help, defend, and pray for his little brother. Then Mark's mother went in the hospital. Between her and Timmy, the family was in the hospital sixteen times in two years. Then Mark's grandma and grandpa died.

That little fellow hurt. He went through pain. But now, if

you compare him with the rest of the nine-year-olds in this country, they're not even in his league. He's major league. They're still in Little League because they haven't experienced suffering. Pain is good.

In verse 13, Solomon gives us a central point.

Consider the work of God,
For who is able to straighten what He has bent?

Solomon reminds us that there are some things we can't change. We just have to trust that they are the work of God.

When you hurt, don't point your finger at God. "And we know that God causes all things to work together for good" (Rom. 8:28). "Rejoice in the Lord always" (Phil. 4:4). Our Lord is in heaven and He does whatever He pleases.

Don't miss the blessing by trying to change what cannot be changed. Stop and reflect on the Word of God. Let God use the pain to change you.

You can change some difficult situations. If you're hurting because of sin, repent! If you're suffering in life because your ear sticks out, get it fixed!

What has God bent? Embrace those things you cannot change as God's plan for your life.

In the day of prosperity be happy,
But in the day of adversity consider—
God has made the one as well as the other
So that man may not discover anything that will be
after him. (v. 14)

Don't go looking for pain. Prosperity can be a blessing from God.

If you're in a time of pain and adversity right now, be patient. A day of prosperity is coming. And if you're in a time of prosperity in which everything is great, start preparing. A day of pain and adversity is just around the corner.

You can't know the future. Solomon's logic is that God doesn't always do what's pleasant for you; He always does what's best.

If God always did what was pleasant, you could know what would come after you. You could know the future. Adversity and prosperity—God brings them both. You can be sure that the future won't be exactly what you hope it will be since prosperity is not the best thing for you and adversity is not the worst. Solomon says that God brings wisdom through pain.

In the next section, Solomon is going to remind us that we need to have a correct perspective of not only adversity but also ourselves. As we will see in the next chapter, a person who hasn't learned humility will always have a problem with God.

For Discussion and Application

1. "We are not impressed by truth. We are shaped by pain." Do you agree or disagree? Why or why not?

2. Have you ever been influenced by foolish friends? What about someone you know or love? How did it happen? What was the result?

3. When have you had an experience like Tommy's that showed that "the end of a matter is better than the beginning"? What happened? What did you learn?

CHAPTER 7

Holiness
and Humility

ECCLESIASTES 7:15–29

How Can I Live in a World Where I Don't Have All the Answers?

In an act of rebellion, a young woman named Rebecca in my church got involved with an abusive man and had a child. She hoped he would become kinder, but the man's abuse got worse and worse. One day he struck her and crushed the side of her face. She had to have reconstructive surgery to repair the damage.

The man left and Rebecca returned to the Lord, serving Him with her whole heart. I recently saw her when she returned from a mission trip to an orphanage in a Muslim country. She had the most wonderful glow on her face. I listened as she told me about her trip. Then I asked her, "Rebecca, what is the passion of your heart?" She looked me in the eye and said with conviction, "Working with abused women."

An Outline of Ecclesiastes
Following the Logic of Solomon
V. Be Correct in Perspective: 5:8–7:29
    Wealth: Don't be deceived when the wicked increase; wealth
       won't satisfy (5:8–6:12).
    Adversity: Hard times are not bad; they shape us (7:1–14).
    Yourself: Be humble; you can't know all things (7:15–29).

"God seeks what is passed by." Her pain worked for her ultimate good.

Consider Moses, who was rescued when all the other Hebrew male babies were killed. Not only was he rescued, but he was reared in Pharaoh's house. He had the best of everything.

When he was forty years old, he lost it all in a fit of anger and had to hide in the desert for forty years. Why would God allow this to happen to him?

Because God used all of it—even the consequences of his sin and the forty years in the desert—to prepare Moses to set His people free.

Have you ever felt like God is having you do things that seem like a waste of time? Sometimes it may even feel like you are going in the wrong direction. But God has to teach you to trust Him, to rest in Him, and to know that His way is best. You need humility as you walk with God. If you trust Him, you'll be willing to let Him put you through some tough times . . . and those times will shape you into a better tool for His work.

I wouldn't repeat my painful times for anything, but I wouldn't trade them for anything either.

Solomon gives us another correction for when we go through hard times. To recap, his previous corrections were (1) prosperity isn't always good and (2) adversity isn't always bad. His third correction is for us to trust God even when things don't add up. We are not omniscient.

*I have seen everything during my lifetime of futility;
there is a righteous man who perishes in his righteousness, and there is a wicked man who prolongs his life
in his wickedness. (v. 15)*

Why did Betsy Ten Boom die in a Nazi concentration camp? This holy heroine, who mentored her sister Corrie, died without a husband or children. If I were God, I would have saved that woman, given her a husband, and let her have fifteen kids all greater than she. Here was this ideal woman who died a horrible death in the most atrocious conditions. Why?

Did you ever see the movie *Chariots of Fire?* Eric Liddell, a godly congregational minister's son, gave up all the wealth he could have earned for winning the 1924 Olympic gold medal in Paris (for the 400-meter race) and became a missionary to China. He was truly a righteous man. And he was a well-loved man. When Liddell left Edinburgh for China the year after winning the gold medal, thousands of people wanting to bid him farewell waited for a glimpse of him as he boarded his ship.

Do you know what happened to Eric Liddell? During World War II, he was taken prisoner with other Westerners and was among the two thousand people crowded into a Japanese internment camp. His cell was three-by-six feet. Before his arrest, Liddell managed to get his wife, Florence, and two children to safety in Canada. (She was pregnant at the time with their third daughter, whom Eric would never see.)

Eric Liddell became ill and died of a brain tumor at the age of forty-two on February 21, 1945.

How can that possibly be? Eric Liddell was a godly man who stood strong for Christ. He loved Christ more than personal gain and stayed devoted to Him even in the face of personal tragedy. If it had been up to me, I would have levitated him up to glory. Wicked men are the ones who should have brain tumors and die at forty-two. Why did it have to happen to Eric Liddell?

That's the way it is sometimes. And if that doesn't stun you, Solomon says that sometimes a person's wickedness is the very thing that prolongs his life. So now we have even more problems with God. But he tells us how we can deal with it.

Do not be excessively righteous, and do not be overly wise. Why should you ruin yourself? (v. 16)

This is an often-misinterpreted verse. I knew a guy who said he was a Christian but was a very ungodly man. This was his life's verse. He knew it in eight translations. "The Bible says don't be overly wise. The Bible says don't be overly holy." Hail mediocrity!

But as Augustine said, we should interpret Scripture by other Scripture. Now, obviously, the Bible teaches us to seek righteousness and holiness. Philippians 3:13–14 says, "One thing I [Paul] do: forgetting what lies behind and reaching forward to what lies ahead, I press on toward the goal for the prize of the upward call of God in Christ Jesus." The Bible calls us to be fervent in our pursuit of wisdom and righteousness—to seek them and not to yield.

Solomon is talking in context about an observer becoming so bent on being holy and informed that he forgets the grace of the all-knowing God. He's talking about pharisaical wisdom and pharisaical righteousness.

He is saying that we shouldn't think we are smart enough and wise enough to understand what God is doing. We can't call God to the bar of human reason. Isaiah 40:13–14 says,

Who has directed the Spirit of the LORD,
Or as His counselor has informed Him?
With whom did He consult and who gave Him
    understanding?
And who taught Him in the path of justice and taught
    Him knowledge,
And informed Him of the way of understanding?

God owes nothing to us and no one completely understands Him. We can only know what God reveals to us about Himself.

God will disappoint our expectations sometime, and we will go off the deep end to our ruin. We will make stupid decisions and abandon our families, throw away our careers, and turn our backs on our good friends—all because we think we are righteous and wise enough to accuse God.

In verse 17, Solomon shows us the peril of going to the opposite extreme.

Do not be excessively wicked, and do not be a fool.
Why should you die before your time?

Bernard, one of my assistants at church, lives on a busy street. Late one night he heard an awful crash and went outside to investigate. He found the wreck of a car that had been carrying three teenagers. They were out late one night, got liquored up, and then flipped their car.

One of the young men wasn't wearing his seat belt. Why should he obey the law? After all, he knew everything and was invincible. When the car flipped, he bounced around so that his head came out the window. The car turned over on him and beheaded him.

Bernard came out to the street and was shocked when he saw the body. He said, "There was this marvelous eighteen-year-old body and it was dead." This young man could have been a husband, a father, a businessman, or a homeowner, and could have enjoyed Rocky Road. He could have gone to the opera. Here's a kid who could have taken a ride in the gondolas of Venice and enjoyed a splendid sunset. He could have married a dear girl and sat in a swing with their child on his lap and listened to the toe-tapping tunes of Bill Gaither.

Instead, he was dead at eighteen, trapped underneath a car with a belly full of beer.

What do you say to that, Solomon? Stupid, that's what he says. So don't think you're smart enough to understand God, but also don't just chuck it all and be a fool. If you make stupid choices, you'll end up suffering the consequences. Now read Solomon's conclusion.

It is good that you grasp one thing, and also not let go of the other; for the one who fears God comes forth with both of them. (v. 18)

The "one thing" that you're to grasp is the teaching of verse 17. "The other" thing that you're not to let go of is the wisdom of verse 16. In other words, it is good in life to grasp verse 17—don't be wicked and foolish and blow life; be holy and wise. But at the same time, remember verse 16—you are a finite sinner who can't control God or even understand what He's up to. Obey God in what you know. Trust Him in what you don't.

Isn't that great? Solomon says that in a life of inequity, you need to live in godly fear of the Lord. While you are growing in faith, make sure that you don't become wise in your own estimation. You need to remember that no matter how righteous you are, you're still a sinner saved by the grace of God.

Jesus Christ came to give us His wisdom, righteousness, holiness, and redemption. Outside of God's grace, you and I haven't got the sense to come in out of the rain, as my momma used to say.

John Newton, the former slave trader and author of "Amazing Grace," said, "When I get to heaven, I will be amazed at three things. I will be amazed at those I thought would be there who are not there, those I did not think would be there who are there, and the fact that I am there at all."

Early in the ministry of the apostle Paul, he called himself the least of the apostles. Later on he said he was the least of all Christians. Then he said he was the chief of sinners. The older he got, the more he saw of God, the lower he became in his own estimation.

So Solomon has given us three corrections. Correction number one: Prosperity is not always best. Correction number two: adversity is not always worst. And correction number three: realize that you don't have the last word on knowledge.

Now Solomon is going to show us how to apply this information.

Wisdom strengthens a wise man more than ten rulers who are in a city. (v. 19)

The wisdom of God is better than surrounding yourself with the ten best men you can find. It's been said that a man with a Bible could stay in a cave for a year, and at the end of that time, he could know (from his reading) what everybody else in the world was doing.

There is no greater blessing than wisdom. There is no greater activity than walking with God and revering Him. But watch out that you don't let your good behavior go to your head.

Indeed, there is not a righteous man on earth who continually does good and who never sins. (v. 20)

When I was in college, we would occasionally have visiting preachers speak to us. Many times, these preachers were into the holiness movement, so they did not sin. We knew they didn't sin because they told us they didn't sin.

They would call all the guys drunks and all the girls whores and declare that every one of us was going to hell. And it seemed like they were glad of those facts.

Even though they did not sin anymore, they looked suspiciously arrogant to me. In fact, if you hear people claim they are the incarnation of wisdom, you can put away your notebook because you won't need to write down any of their "insight."

Solomon says it is good for you to be in the Word. Stay in the Bible and you'll be on a path to joy and peace, walking with God. It's good to be wise in that way.

As a matter of fact, no matter how many degrees you have, if you don't soak in the Bible, you're stumbling through a minefield. If all you know is the wisdom of the Bible and you don't have a degree, you'll still have a joyful, happy life. Now, you may not have a jet ski, but can you live with that?

Wisdom is better than ten rulers. You can surround yourself with the greatest men, but if you know and fear God, you're ahead of the pack.

So it's good to be wise, but make sure you temper it by being downwind of yourself. Don't focus on the fact that you are rising above the people around you. Look at Jesus Christ and let Him be your standard.

One of the most important aspects of wisdom is being able to deal with sin in a fallen world.

Dealing with the Sin of Others and Ourselves
Also, do not take seriously all words which are spoken, lest you hear your servant cursing you. (v. 21)

Solomon says to not be amazed or go into a depression when you encounter your sin. Don't be surprised that some people don't like you. And don't be surprised that, because of your sin, some of them have a good reason to dislike you!

It's been said that great men are never great to their valets. Servants always know the worst side of their employers. Who do we tend to treat in a special way? People who are above us in power, prestige, or rank. Who do we treat like dirt? People who are beneath us in some sense.

And when you discover that someone (servant or not) has said something negative about you, note your initial reaction. Is it to get defensive and angry with the other person? Or do you consider that, even though the person was wrong to gossip, there may be some grounds for what was said?

And the reason you can be sure that someone is talking about you is that you have talked about others. We all have dark sides.

For you also have realized that you likewise have many times cursed others. (v. 22)

You have cursed many people in your lifetime, haven't you? Do you know why you've said things to them and about them? Because both of you are sinners.

Solomon is telling us this fact about ourselves and others to substantiate what he said about how to live in a fallen world. Here's how: Realize that we don't know everything, then strive for holiness and hold on to the fact that we're sinners just like the rest of humanity. That's why we talk trash about others. We know no perfect people.

We have to go beyond just saying we are sinners to really believing at our core that we are completely dependent on God's grace. If you knew about me what God knows, you wouldn't have bought this book. And if I knew of you what God knows, I probably wouldn't let you read it. We're all sinners.

Solomon brings this point home through his personal experience.

> I tested all this with wisdom, and I said, "I will be wise," but it was far from me. What has been is remote and exceedingly mysterious. Who can discover it? I directed my mind to know, to investigate, and to seek wisdom and an explanation, and to know the evil of folly and the foolishness of madness. And I discovered more bitter than death the woman whose heart is snares and nets, whose hands are chains. One who is pleasing to God will escape from her, but the sinner will be captured by her. (vv. 23–26)

Solomon takes a turn here and talks again about his own experience. He says that he made a commitment to be a holy man, but he couldn't come close. This is a precursor to Romans 7:24, where Paul asks, "Who will set me free from the body of this death?" Solomon is saying that he could not find righteousness on his own.

Nothing is more comforting than the doctrine of total depravity. In fact, the doctrine of total depravity is the most emotionally freeing doctrine in all of New Testament theology. It states that my whole person has been radically tainted by sin. Everything I can do, think, or say on this side of glory will be tainted by sin. In our fallen state, our entire will is oriented against God. We are bent on our own ways of evil from the get-go.

Augustine said the only reason you think a baby is good is

that he hasn't got power enough to show you how evil he is. He said, "If a baby had the strength when he emerged from the mother's womb, he would seize the mother by the throat and demand his milk."

The only way any of us can be saved is if God makes a radical change in us from the inside out. So Jesus gave Himself as a sacrifice for our sins. Then the Spirit of God changes our nature by abiding with us, keeping us, sanctifying us, and raising us by His power.

The doctrine of depravity is comforting because it means sanctification is not up to me. You may be surprised that you're evil, but it is no revelation to God. Hallelujah!

Solomon says that the past is unknowable by us, but it is part of God's sovereign design. We cannot know the mind of God. It is exceedingly mysterious. We don't have a clue as to what God is doing.

In verse 25, Solomon says, "I want to prove it to you." He investigated and sought out any explanation for these matters. And he learned that it is better to be wise and righteous than to be a sinner. He gives a practical example of being smart and holy in verse 26. Mind you, he's warning both sexes to watch out for people (not just women) whose hearts are snares and whose hands are chains.

Human sexuality has been an area of temptation and sin since the Fall of man. Even though God doesn't tell us everything, He does tell us to be sexually pure. So many people today are not willing to experience short-term frustration to achieve long-term pleasure. Instead, they hop in the sack with anyone that says a kind word to them and end up destroying their lives and families.

Believe me, I understand that sex is fun. But I also know that outside of marriage, sex is playing with fire. It will burn down your house and consume you. Don't buy into some short-term pleasure that will leave you a lifetime of pain.

If you are single and reading this book, you may long to experience physical intimacy. If you are married, you may want your sex life to be better than it is. In either case, you may wonder why God doesn't fix things and make everything OK.

Don't let what you can't understand negate what you can do right now. You don't have to figure out the universe. Solomon says that even though he can't understand God, here is one thing he is sure of: It's better to do the right thing. Be pure.

You don't have to be omniscient to be happy. What you do have to do is defend your six square feet of ground with the wisdom you're given.

To figure out life, I don't need to know what God's doing. What I do need to do is avoid evil and do right and please God. For everything else, let the chips fall where they may and don't worry.

God will do His job in directing the universe; we can be sure of that. The question is, Will you do your job? Your job is to be honest, holy, loving, and righteous and to die well.

In verses 27 and 28, Solomon explains another discovery. Even though we seek righteousness, we need to remember that no matter how good we get, we are sinful. All of us. Men and women both. We need to remember that no matter how good we get, the only reason people tolerate us is that we have learned how to tame our public evil as opposed to our private evil. Does that disturb you about yourself? Here it is again: The only reason that you're a likeable person is that you have learned to distinguish between your public and private obnoxiousness, and you are smart enough to keep your lustful, hateful, wicked thoughts contained in your brain. In your public treatment of people, you have remained basically hygienic and nonviolent.

"Behold, I have discovered this," says the Preacher,
"adding one thing to another to find an explanation,
which I am still seeking but have not found. I have
found one man among a thousand, but I have not
found a woman among all these." (vv. 27–28)

If you are a woman, don't throw this book in the fireplace and use it for kindling. Let me tell you what verse 28 means. Solomon is using hyperbole. He doesn't have anything good to say about men or women. It's a poetic statement. Among a thousand men he's found one good guy but hasn't found a good woman yet. It's hyperbole for the fact that we're all a bunch of sinners. Recall Romans 3:23—"All have sinned and fall short of the glory of God." Ecclesiastes 7:29 says Solomon may not have discovered all the answers, but he has discovered this: Men are definitely fallen.

How do we live in light of these truths? Apply wisdom where you are. Seek God to know Him. Trust Him. Grow in Him; but remember that you are a sinner, you live among sinners, and you have no wisdom in yourself.

You wouldn't even recognize God unless He provided Christ and the Holy Spirit drew you and converted you. You'd still be dead in sin unless Christ's righteousness was imputed to you. It's only on the basis of His death that God forgave you. And it's by His grace that He keeps you.

He did not choose you because you moved an inch toward Him but because you're the weakest of all people. "See how great a love the Father has bestowed upon us" (1 John 3:1). He did not give us what we deserve. He bestowed mercy. That is a freeing doctrine.

You need to grow. Don't do things to shoot yourself in the foot. You can't control the sovereignty of God in this universe.

But you can control whether you are an obnoxious person nobody likes. Seek God, defend your ground, be holy, and don't worry about Him; He'll take care of you.

As you grow, do not let the grace of God go sour on you. Let me explain what I mean. I had a buddy who was one of the first guys to share the gospel with me. In high school, he talked to me about Christ. I didn't get it until years later when I finally trusted Christ.

This friend of mine got married. Then he went through a divorce. He turned his back on God and fell into sin, repented, and got married again. We were still friends through all this. In fact, I was the best man at his second wedding.

Then you know what he did? He left his wife and lived with another woman. I sat him down and rebuked him. He protested, "I finally met a woman who can teach me how to love." I looked at him and said, "You don't have a brain in your head. What are you thinking?" I did everything but punch him out. I loved him but I was so mad at him. He knew I loved him, so he listened to my preaching at him.

Later on, he went on some retreat, had a religious experience, and came back as a "spiritual man." He'd learned the secret truths of what it meant to be a *real* Christian and he had "arrived." I was still stuck in Getting It, Texas, with a Bible.

You know what he did? He preached at me. It seems he knew it all. He was the self-righteous player on the varsity team, and I was only JV.

You know what I said to him? I put my hands on his shoulders, looked him in the eyes, and said, "I liked you better when you were an adulterer. At least you were humble." A wise man is righteous, but he doesn't let go of the fact that he is a sinner. Don't ever think you've arrived, or God's grace will go sour.

I've seen men and women who don't know much about theology start reading about it. They read a little Francis Schaeffer and C. S. Lewis. They learn a little baby Greek. All of the sudden, you can't stand to be around them and their pontificating.

They go rancid. They sour. It's called grace going putrid. They've gotten so high toward God that they can't see anything but themselves.

"God, I thank Thee that I am not like other people: swindlers, unjust, adulterers, or even like this tax gatherer. I fast twice a week; I pay tithes of all that I get" (Luke 18:11–12). The Pharisee didn't say one lie in his prayer. Everything he said was true about himself and about the other man. But there's something about that prayer that stinks: He forgot who he was before God. That's grace gone sour.

I've seen guys who start reading their Bibles and then pick up Jonathan Edwards, R. C. Sproul, and John Owen. All of a sudden, they have a theological epiphany. Before you know it, they're condescending toward every mortal Christian.

Don't let grace go sour on you. C. S. Lewis says that God always gives us struggles in life. He makes sure that we always are facing things we can't quite figure out. And the reason He does it is so we will remember that this world is not our home. If you have a good meal, if you have an enjoyable recreational activity, if you have a sweet time with your spouse, that's good. But God will always let you know that this world is just an inn. We are just passing through. It's not a destination; it's a motel. God will not let your life get so solid that you can trust in your family, your health, your talent, your friends, or your church—not completely. He wants us to enjoy those things but to put our trust completely in Him.

A good question to ask at this point is, What does it look like to trust in God in hard times? That's exactly what Solomon covers in the next section of Ecclesiastes.

For Discussion and Application

1. Why do you think it is so easy for us to have a higher opinion of ourselves than we should? What are some of the motivations that lie behind this?

2. Has there been a time in your life when you were overwhelmed by someone's sin against you? Does it help to remember that you have also sinned against others? Why or why not?

3. What does Tommy mean when he says, "Don't let what you can't figure out deter you from what you already know to be true," particularly in the context of verses 25 and 26?

4. Why does Tommy say that total depravity is one of the most freeing doctrines in the Bible? Is there a wrong way to take this? What would that look like? What is the right way to understand it?

CHAPTER 8

Poise *in* Life

ECCLESIASTES 8:1–9:1

How Should I Act When There Doesn't Seem to Be Any Way to Win in Life?

One time a few friends and I flew in a small plane to the town of Lake Placid, Florida. The plane was an old "prop job," and in the middle of the flight, we got socked in by a wall of clouds. Vertigo came over me, and I didn't know if I was up, down, or sideways. I looked at the man next to me, and he was sweating.

I said, "What direction does it feel like we're flying to you?"

He said, "I don't know, but I think we're upside down."

By that time, I felt like we were flying straight for the ground.

Then I looked at the pilot, an old guy who wore a leather hat with flaps on his head and a big white kerchief around his neck. While I was scared stiff, he was whistling and having a good time.

I said, "Don't these clouds make it hard for you to see where we're going?"

An Outline of Ecclesiastes
Following the Logic of Solomon
VI. Be Courageous in Life: 8:1–12:8
    Be bold in doing right even if you're not rewarded (8:1–10:20).

He said, "Oh yeah, when I look out the window, I can't tell anything about where I'm headed."

"Why aren't you a little more concerned, then?"

He pointed down to the gauges on the panel. "See this right here? It never lies. We're right here. There's a Delta plane over there and an American plane over there. The ground is down here. I know who's talking to me on the radio; it's Leonard from Fort Myers. I know right where I am."

That's exactly how life is sometimes. We get enveloped in suffering and don't know which way is up. If we looked at the circumstances around us, we'd end up chucking all reason and flying straight into the ground.

When we don't know what's going on, we have to fly by the panel. You don't abandon your faith because you can't figure it out. You don't punt because God didn't behave. You trust in what you know, not in how you feel. That's flying by the panel.

I recently visited with Tammy, a young lady who had moved away from Denton. I had counseled her often when she was a member of my church. She had mangled many of the important relationships in her life, and it was tough to connect with her. She could be clingy and codependent. I always had to weigh my words carefully when I spoke with her because her feelings were so easily hurt.

Why was Tammy this way? Early in her life, something bad had happened that she couldn't understand. Someone had sinned against her, and she had never recovered. She could never fully believe that God could heal her and take care of her. She could never be still and know that He was God. She could never "in everything give thanks; for this is God's will for you in Christ Jesus" (1 Thess. 5:18). Tammy could never say, "all things work together for good" (Rom. 8:28). She could never fly by the panel. Her circumstances were sovereign.

We've all known people like this. Maybe you have been a person like this at one time, or maybe you are right now.

Many times in our lives we will go through things we can't understand. How do we become the kind of people who can graciously endure the knocks and bumps of life? How do we remember our smallness and God's greatness? How do you fly by the panel?

Solomon teaches us how to survive in a fallen world. In chapter 6 of Ecclesiastes, he tells us that evil people may prosper, but that doesn't mean they're happy. In chapter 7, he reminds us that suffering is not the worst thing that can happen to us.

In chapter 8 of Ecclesiastes, Solomon shows us that wisdom endures even when it doesn't understand. Life is not fair, and God almost never gives us answers.

Solomon emphasizes the importance of poise in the face of trials. Do you know what poise means? It's related to the word "pose"—to freeze and not move. A "posit" is a truth you believe and hold onto. Poise means that you don't shift due to outside circumstances.

Let me give you an example from sports. If you're a shortstop and you make an error in the ninth inning of a tie game, allowing a runner to move to third base, you've got to put that blunder behind you. When there are two outs and the ball is hit to you, poise means that you put aside the noise of the crowd and your disappointment about the earlier error. You just make the play you're supposed to make. You focus on the fundamentals and act according to the rules of the position. You're not manipulated or intimidated by any forces from outside of you. You do exactly what a shortstop should do. You approach the ball. You take the hop. You come up throwing, hit the first baseman right in the letters, and get the out because you have poise.

Do you know some Christians who, when things didn't work out, got rattled and lost their faith? When we lose our trust in God, we become like Tammy from my church—a walking sore that infects everyone around us.

Chapter 8 of Ecclesiastes applies to every one of us. Watch and learn from what Solomon says about poise. In verse 1 he asserts that the best thing we can have in life is wisdom—to know the will of God:

Who is like the wise man and who knows the interpretation of a matter? A man's wisdom illumines him and causes his stern face to beam.

What authority is intelligent enough to be compared with a person who has a Bible in his hand and who knows God's will? Solomon says the wise person is illumined and has so much joy that you can see it on his face.

Do you have joy? If not, perhaps it's because you aren't soaking in the wisdom of God's Word. It's not being integrated into your life and giving you poise.

Wisdom brings poise because a person who has biblical wisdom is assured of what is right. There is no greater privilege than understanding where we came from, who we are, where we are going, how sin is removed, and what the will of God is. There is no greater blessing. And there is no other place to find these answers than from God in His Word.

Solomon begins this chapter by saying that in a world full of questions, it's wonderful to know the absolutes of life. Some things in life we can't understand but some things we can understand—what the moral will of God is, who He is, and who we are in Him.

So whenever you run up against inequity in life, don't rebel.

I say, "Keep the command of the king because of the oath before God. Do not be in a hurry to leave him. Do not join in an evil matter, for he will do whatever he pleases." Since the word of the king is authoritative, who will say to him, "What are you doing?" He who keeps a royal command experiences no trouble, for a wise heart knows the proper time and procedure. (vv. 2–5)

The command of the king was meant to be obeyed because he was under the leadership of God. The Jewish people swore an oath of allegiance and obedience to the king. Solomon is reminding us that we are called to obey authority. Don't abandon that position. Even if you have an evil king, don't panic.

For the Israelites, to leave the king was to commit treason. Just because a king is not doing what you think he should do, don't be in a hurry to disobey. Every time a person in the Old Testament rebelled against the king, he ended up being killed.

Nobody can challenge the king; he will do what he pleases. It takes patience and trust in God to submit to frail, human authority.

Who is the greatest example in the Bible of a young man who endured an evil king? One time when the king was trying to kill him, the young man had the opportunity to kill the king. I'm referring to David and King Saul.

David wouldn't kill Saul because of the oath he had given to God: "I will not stretch out my hand against . . . the Lord's anointed" (1 Sam. 24:10). David would not be ruled by his feelings, circumstances, or peers. David chose to be ruled only by the will of God.

That is poise. When you're in a cave and the man who is trying to kill you relieves himself and is within your reach, it takes poise not to take him out. Even though God had ordained David to be king some day, he didn't take matters into his own hands.

You can't control everything in life and that's OK. Obey the moral will of God and do what He commands you to do. Solomon says the obedient man can obey and know that no troubles will follow. He "experiences no trouble."

If your life is characterized by submission and obedience, there will be a "proper time and procedure" for dealing with problems. When you're obeying the will of God, you don't have to worry.

Are you spending time with God? Are you walking with God? Are you serving Him? Are you sharing His Word? Are you in the will of God? Are you doing well with the things that are in your control? Then don't worry about the things you can't control.

When was the last time you lied to manipulate your circumstances? What's one of the problems with lying? Remembering your lie. When you lie, you have two alternative universes: the universe you are in and the universe that you created in the other person's mind when you lied.

Imagine telling someone you were a two-time All-American at LSU, when in reality you got cut as a walk-on at Nicholls State. Then you tell someone else that you had an offer from the Padres right out of high school. Sometimes you get them mixed up: Is that the LSU person, or is that the Padres person?

Do you see what happens? Sin is like potato chips; you can never eat just one. Once you sin, inevitably you'll be tempted to sin more to cover it up. If you steal something, you have to lie and hide it from your family. If you cheat the government, you have to lie and keep covering your phony tax tracks. If you

cheat on your wife, you'll always wonder if she smells the for-
eign perfume.

But the truth is that you don't have to lie and sin to make
your situation better. God will make things right in His good
time. God can change everything at the proper time through His
procedures.

A great example of this is Belshazzar, the king of Persia—
one of the most wicked rulers in the Old Testament. Daniel tells
how Belshazzar took the cups and articles from the temple in
Jerusalem and used them to mock God. He praised the gods of
stone and gold and silver and earth.

In Persia, whenever a king wrote an edict, it couldn't be
changed. One night at a party, this human king saw a hand writing on the wall. It was an immortal hand, a deathless hand. The
very hand of God was writing something unchangeable:
"MENĒ, MENĒ, TEKĒL, UPHARSIN" (Dan. 5:25), which
means that Belshazzar had been weighed in the balance and had
been found wanting. His kingdom would be taken away and
given to the Medes and the Persians. And the writing came true:
that very night, his kingdom collapsed.

Can God take out a wicked ruler anytime He wants to? Yes,
He can.

Nicolae Ceausescu was born in Romania in 1918. A devout
communist, he was imprisoned for his beliefs in 1936 and 1940.
After the communists took control of Romania in 1947,
Ceausescu quickly moved up the political ranks until he became
the head of state in 1967. He ruled Romania with an iron hand
for more than twenty years.

On December 17, 1989, Ceausescu ordered army troops to
fire on a crowd of civilian protesters in Timosora. They refused.
Over the next few days, protests spread throughout the country
and into the capital of Bucharest.

The last speech Ceausescu made was captured on video. He was talking to a crowd in a public square when the protesters overwhelmed his message. In the video, you can see from the look in his eyes that he knew his situation was hopeless. He and his wife tried to flee the city in a helicopter, but they were caught.

The next video footage of the revolution shows two policemen walking Ceausescu and his wife outside and lining them up against a wall. Then you hear, "Pop, pop, pop, pop, pop," and the screen fills with smoke. In the next scene, a doctor is feeling for Ceausescu's pulse. The video lasts about three minutes. The events themselves occurred in less than five days. That's how quickly God can take out an evil man.

A wise man knows God can change things in a heartbeat. Anytime God wants to, He can turn your world upside down. So a wise man rests in the sovereignty of God, rather than taking matters in his own hands. In verse 6 Solomon offers a general principle.

For there is a proper time and procedure for every delight, when a man's trouble is heavy upon him.

When my life is burdensome and my heart is broken, I need to remember that there is a proper time and procedure for every delight. There will be a time when this trouble is gone. There will be times of laughter. In God's purposes, there will be a time when everything is turned upright again.

So if you have trouble that is heavy on you right now, know that it's all in the sovereign purposes of God. Change what you can change. Be wise. But in what you can't change, rest in the sovereignty of God.

Let me ask you a very penetrating question: If you're going through great struggles right now, how much of your difficulties involves things you can't change and how much involves things you can? Verse 6 indicates that you need not worry about the things you can't change. Rest in the sovereignty of God. The things you can change, you need to change. For the others, let God's wisdom illumine you.

In verse 7, Solomon reminds us that God makes time, but men make watches.

If no one knows what will happen, who can tell him when it will happen?

Don't keep a stopwatch on God. Don't put Him on your timetable so that He has to perform.

Remain poised. Keep going to church, keep singing, and keep listening. Take the first fruits of your wealth and give them to the Lord. Spend time every day in your Bible and prayer. Check yourself for moral purity. Guard your tongue. Look at the relationships you have and ask yourself if you are sharing the gospel. These are things you can control and in which your wisdom can make your stern face beam. Be illumined by them.

On the things you can't control, you can rest. You can just chill. You can wait because you know that when you're in trouble, there's a proper time and procedure for every delight. Joseph waited thirteen years; Abraham, twenty-five; Jacob, twenty. The saints of Hebrews 11 waited a lifetime then *died* in faith not receiving the promise! (Heb. 11:39–40)

Right now, I could tell you about three or four things in my life that could easily keep me awake at night. I don't see hope for any of them.

But you know what? They aren't keeping me awake because I'm not worried about what's going to happen. The reason I'm not worried is that I know I'm not in control. If the results depended on me, I'd be worried sick. But it's not up to me, it's up to God, and He's a lot more dependable than I am.

Some of these situations are sinful things that others have done to me, and I do wish God would hit some of them with a meteor. But no cosmic shower has occurred and that's OK.

Here's what I know: I read my Bible this morning and I'm trying to live by it. I loved my wife today and I was affectionate to her. I haven't slandered anybody yet today.

I'm happy and yet I've got struggles. Those are God's business. Is my trouble heavy on me? In a sense it is, but I'm not worried, because there's a proper time and procedure for every delight. I know who holds tomorrow even if I don't know what tomorrow holds.

Do you believe the same?

In verse 8, Solomon shows us that evil men don't have the ability to control their own destinies.

No man has authority to restrain the wind with the wind, or authority over the day of death; and there is no discharge in the time of war, and evil will not deliver those who practice it.

Perhaps the most evil of the Old Testament kings, next to Manasseh, was Ahab. He married a Phoenician woman named Jezebel. He brought idolatry into Israel and God didn't do anything about it. He authorized Jezebel to kill the prophets of God and she did. Still God didn't act.

Then Ahab tried to kill Elijah. God shut the heavens for a three-and-a-half-year drought, and he still didn't repent.

Ahab longed for the land of a man named Naboth, so he

killed him to take his land. Then Ahab went to battle and had an alliance with a king named Jehoshaphat. They formed a coalition to fight against the Syrians.

Micaiah the prophet had just prophesied that Ahab was going to die, but Ahab was so arrogant, he thought he could cheat death. He told Jehoshaphat to dress like a king, while Ahab dressed in the common gear of a foot soldier. He thought he had outsmarted God.

The Bible says that as the battle began to rage, a Syrian took an arrow and fired it at random in the air. He was probably some scared first-year Syrian soldier stuck in the back of the line, but he let an arrow fly and guess what? It hit Ahab exactly in the exposed joint of his armor.

Ahab told his men he was wounded, and they took him in his chariot from the battle. Before he left, he saw his army being destroyed. That was the last thing he remembered as he lost consciousness.

Ahab died in the chariot. When they washed his blood out, the dogs came and licked it up.

Isn't that incredible? As Jonathan Edwards said, God holds evil men like little spiders over the fire. He will let them kick and thrash until He is tired of using them for His purposes. Then He drops them in the flames. When God wanted Ahab out, he was dog food, just like that.

> *All this I have seen and applied my mind to every deed that has been done under the sun wherein a man has exercised authority over another man to his hurt.*
>
> *So then, I have seen the wicked buried, those who used to go in and out from the holy place, and they are soon forgotten in the city where they did thus. This too is futility. (vv. 9–10)*

Solomon says that he learned a long time ago that evil does not ultimately win. God can take it out whenever He pleases. God can do whatever He wants with an evil government. We need to keep our poise when evil is in authority.

Verse 10 creates some problems for translators and commentators. Some say it is the wicked who used to go in and out from the holy place. Others say there should be a period after "buried," implying that both the wicked and the righteous are forgotten. But whichever interpretation you choose, the end is the same. Men are forgotten, and we can't control the sovereignty of God.

> *Because the sentence against an evil deed is not executed quickly, therefore the hearts of the sons of men among them are given fully to do evil. (v. 11)*

The sons of men (also known as the "sons of Adam"—fallen man—as noted in earlier chapters) are people who don't know God. They are at the mercy of their own ignorance. Because a person doesn't see instantaneous justice by God against evil, he thinks he can do evil and get away with it. This same thought is found in 2 Peter 3:3–4, "Mockers will come with their mocking, following after their own lusts, and saying, 'Where is the promise of His coming? For ever since the fathers fell asleep, all continues just as it was from the beginning of creation.'"

But we learned earlier in Ecclesiastes that God's patience is a great blessing. If He were to immediately judge evil, every one of us would have already been condemned.

God is long-suffering and patient because He's gathering His people.

Let me give you an example. At the edge of my church's parking lot is a tree that has thorns around it. One of the people who cares for the church's facilities saw the thorns and intended to use a weed eater to clean around the tree. What he didn't know is that I had planted some tulip bulbs around that very tree.

When I saw him going outside with the weed eater, I stopped him and asked him what he was doing. He said, "I'm going to take those thorns out from around that tree." I said, "Now, wait just a minute. You don't know where my tulips are." I told him to let the briars grow because in among them are my tulips. As soon as the tulips grow tall, we can clip them and put them in a beautiful vase. Then he can weed-eat those briars to his heart's content.

There's wickedness in this world and God lets it go on. Do you know why? Because there are also little tulips coming up, and someday He's going to take them away and put them on display in glory. Then He will have at those briars.

So be of good cheer. That's why God doesn't remove every hindrance quickly. God wants us to walk by faith.

Another great example of poise comes from the Book of Daniel. Shadrach, Meshach, and Abed-nego were told they must bow down to idols. They refused and were thrown into a fiery furnace. How's that for an unjust situation?

They could have chucked their beliefs and bowed to the idol to keep out of the furnace. Instead, they said to the king who had issued the edict for everyone to bow to an idol, "O Nebuchadnezzar, we do not need to give you an answer concerning this matter. If it be so, our God whom we serve is able to deliver us from the furnace of blazing fire; and He will deliver us out of your hand, O king. But even if He does not, let it be known to you, O king, that we are not going to serve your gods or worship the golden image that you have set up" (Dan. 3:16–18).

They were willing to trust God no matter the outcome.

Before Thomas Cranmer was burned at the stake by "Bloody Mary," the Catholic Queen of England, he was told to sign a document to recant his Protestant belief in salvation by faith alone. He had already signed a document before that recanted his position, but he had professed his faith again and was now going to his death for his beliefs.

As the wood was piled around him and the fire was set and began to burn, his accusers came to him, released his right hand from his bonds and placed a quill pen in it, and gave him one last chance to sign the document that would have recanted his Protestant position on salvation by faith alone.

Instead of signing the document, he took his right hand— the hand that had signed the earlier recantation—and held it in the flames until it burned off. He said, "So be it to the hand that offended me." Now, that's poise.

I've got a friend who had a little brother named Tommy, who loved the Lord. When Tommy died of leukemia, it broke my friend's heart and his parents' hearts and crushed his family.

My friend's name was Joe; he was a Marine and loved to control things. He said that for a brief period of time, he was so bitter toward God that he dropped out of church and stopped reading his Bible.

Then one day, he says, it was just like the hand of God touched him with wisdom. He said to himself, "No matter what happened and no matter what I can't understand, there is an infinite, personal God who gave His Son to die, who saved me by faith, who in His Word shows me how to live holy, and who promises me a revelation at the end of the Bible where evil is judged and good is rewarded." He decided to trust God. That's what you call poise.

You will have to decide on your poise some day. You may have to bury a child. Your heart will break, and you will wonder why; but you will hear nothing but a faint, mocking echo of your own words. God will not give you reasons, and you'll have to rest in that silence. Remember Ecclesiastes 8:5—"He who keeps a royal command experiences no trouble." There is a proper time for every delight when evil rests heavy on a man.

Solomon continues his thoughts.

Although a sinner does evil a hundred times and may lengthen his life, still I know that it will be well for those who fear God, who fear Him openly. But it will not be well for the evil man and he will not lengthen his days like a shadow, because he does not fear God. There is futility which is done on the earth, that is, there are righteous men to whom it happens according to the deeds of the wicked. On the other hand, there are evil men to whom it happens according to the deeds of the righteous. I say that this too is futility. (vv. 12–14)

Though 7:15 speaks of times when an evil man may have a prolonged life, generally the evil man's life won't come to a peaceful end. What goes around will come around. Someday evil or justice will catch up with him; we just can't be sure when.

But in the meantime, life will not appear just. The righteous will suffer in the short term and the wicked will prosper.

Tammy, whom I mentioned at the opening of this chapter, is obsessed with things she can't understand. Who knows why she was abused when she was twelve? Can anybody tell me why God would allow that? I don't know. You don't know. Tammy doesn't know. And we'll never know. But instead of remaining poised, obeying the command, trusting God, and working through her pain, Tammy simply abandoned her faith. So now she just hurts and has no hope at all.

So what can you do? Do right. Trust God. Remain poised. Be a Joseph, a Daniel, or an Abraham. And in verse 15 Solomon reminds us again that we should enjoy right now. Don't let what you can't control tomorrow ruin today.

> So I commended pleasure, for there is nothing good
> for a man under the sun except to eat and to drink
> and to be merry, and this will stand by him in his toils
> throughout the days of his life which God has given
> him under the sun.
>   When I gave my heart to know wisdom and to see
> the task which has been done on the earth (even
> though one should never sleep day or night), and I
> saw every work of God, I concluded that man cannot
> discover the work which has been done under the sun.
> Even though man should seek laboriously, he will not
> discover; and though the wise man should say, "I
> know," he cannot discover. (vv. 15–17)

Solomon simply says he tried his best to figure out the inequality of life. He couldn't understand it and you won't be able to either. Even if we never slept and did nothing but investigate and analyze, we would still be left in the dark. It is certain that God is good and true. It is equally certain that life will be enigmatic.

It's foolish to go through life letting your happiness wax and wane according to the circumstances. Solomon again says our response should be to get two dips of Rocky Road—to enjoy life. Don't let what you cannot understand destroy what you can enjoy and what you know to be true.

Let's break into chapter 9 to finish Solomon's thought.

For I have taken all this to my heart and explain it that righteous men, wise men, and their deeds are in the hand of God. Man does not know whether it will be love or hatred; anything awaits him. (v. 1)

I wish I could tell you that if you would just go to church, read your Bible, or send money to my ministry, nothing evil would ever happen to you. But I can't. As a matter of fact, the current "God wants you to be prosperous" and "Bad things can't happen to Christians" idea is incorrect, cruel, and dangerous. God is not that easy to understand.

Solomon says all men are in the hand of God. He is sovereign and doesn't let us in on all of His plans. But we can be sure that He is a loving Father who will never forsake us.

Martin Luther was a German monk who took his religious duties very seriously. He felt the weight of his sin and guilt and worked as hard as he could to earn the favor of God. As a professor at Wittenberg University, he began to read and study. One day he read the text where Jesus Christ said on the cross, "My God, My God, why hast Thou forsaken Me?" Luther could not understand it.

In all of his monastic life, he had tried to earn heaven by his good deeds. Why did evil crush Jesus—someone who had done no wrong? The simple truth of salvation through the cross that you and I rejoice in, he couldn't understand. Why did this perfect man have to die? Why?

Later on, Luther came to the Book of Romans and saw that "the righteousness of God is revealed from faith to faith" (1:17). Luther finally understood that the righteousness of God comes by faith alone. He understood that men are not righteous because they earn the righteousness of God, but because the righteousness of God is given to man through the death and resurrection of Jesus Christ.

Suddenly it all fit together for Luther. Jesus was forsaken so that God in His infinite wisdom could save sinners. Christ died for our sins as a perfect man so that God's wrath would be satisfied.

Martin Luther bowed his head and trusted Christ for his salvation. He said he had such great joy that it was as if he had entered into the very gates of heaven.

Have faith in your loving Father, who gave up His own Son to be reconciled to you, proving His ultimate lasting love for you regardless of what current difficulties may cause you to think. Obey what you know to obey, enjoy what you can enjoy and, for the rest, wait on the timing and purposes of God. When life throws you into a bank of clouds, be sure and fly by the panel.

For Discussion and Application

1. What do you think of when you hear the word "poise"? What does it look like to have poise in the face of struggles?

2. Has there been a time in your life when delayed punishment caused you to sink deeper into sin? What happened? How long did you get away with it? What happened when you were finally found out?

3. What would enable you to trust God in spite of your circumstances? What keeps you from trusting Him? How do you think you can grow in your faith and trust?

CHAPTER 9

Navigating Life's *Winding* Road

ECCLESIASTES 9:2–18

If God Is in Control, Why Does Life Seem to Be So Random?

In 1882, Paul Gauguin lived with his wife and five children in Paris. He was doing well as a thirty-five-year-old stockbroker when he met someone who changed his life—Camille Pisarro. Pisarro was one of the most important artists in the Impressionist movement and had a profound effect on Gauguin. After this friendship blossomed, Gauguin gave up his job to become a devoted art collector and amateur artist.

Three years later, Gauguin abandoned his family. He renounced the trappings of modern life and industrialized society. He first went to the rustic villages of Brittany. In 1891, he went to Tahiti to paint, hoping to find man in pristine innocence there. He believed that in Tahiti there would be no need for rules or religion—nothing to curtail the noble savage. He was hoping to find true beauty and purity.

An Outline of Ecclesiastes
Following the Logic of Solomon
VI. Be Courageous in Life: 8:1–12:8
    Be bold in doing right even if you're not rewarded (8:1–10:20).

What Gauguin found instead was sin, violence, disease, death, pain, and heartache. He discovered there was no such thing as a Shangri-La. He could not find an Oz. He could not find utopia. In response, he tried unsuccessfully to kill himself.

One of the things that I love about the three-thousand-year-old Book of Ecclesiastes is that it does not pretend that life is always nice or fair. Even though a sovereign God directs the world, His ways are unfathomable. God owes no man. He doesn't rely upon anyone. He does what He pleases.

Gauguin could not deal with this fact. He wanted to live life on his terms. He wanted the world to live up to his expectations. But God doesn't play that way.

In chapters 6 through 8 of Ecclesiastes, Solomon gives us perspective as believers. He tells us that good times don't always make us happy and that suffering makes us grow. He tells us to watch our attitude in hard times because we're not all wise and we don't know what is best for us. And he told us that when life doesn't cooperate, we have to fly by the panel. We have to keep walking by faith and remain poised.

In chapter 9, Solomon continues giving us advice about how to make it in this world.

> It is the same for all. There is one fate for the righteous and for the wicked; for the good, for the clean, and for the unclean; for the man who offers a sacrifice and for the one who does not sacrifice. As the good man is, so is the sinner; as the swearer is, so is the one who is afraid to swear. This is an evil in all that is done under the sun, that there is one fate for all men. Furthermore, the hearts of the sons of men are full of evil, and insanity is in their hearts throughout their lives. Afterwards they go to the dead. (vv. 2–3)

In a game of chess, different pieces occupy squares all over the board. The pawns, bishops, rooks, knights, queens, and kings have different abilities and positions of power. But at the end of the game, where do all the pieces end up? In a box.

Solomon says that life is the same way. The righteous and the unrighteous, the moral and the immoral, the goody-two-shoes and the low-down, no-good, egg-sucking dog—they all die. Every last one of them will end up in a box.

Some will die late, some early. But it's the same for both.

Not only that, but Solomon says that during our lives we live among crazy people. Their hearts are so confused that they pursue all kinds of wickedness.

The Calvin and Hobbes comic is one my favorite theological commentaries. In one strip, Calvin says to Hobbes, "Do you think babies are born into the world as sinners?" Hobbes replies, "No, I think they're just quick studies."

Solomon says that the craziness of life makes evil men more evil. One day, some maniac who doesn't have any insurance may run a red light and plow into your car. Or your car might be broken into in a parking lot and your purse will get stolen. Friends will turn their backs on you and say all kinds of terrible things. A customer of your business will get angry, curse you to your face, and then complain to your boss.

How do we live in this world and still believe in a sovereign God? Solomon gives us some insight in the following verses.

For whoever is joined with all the living, there is hope; surely a live dog is better than a dead lion. For the living know they will die; but the dead do not know anything, nor have they any longer a reward, for their memory is forgotten. Indeed their love, their hate, and

*their zeal have already perished, and they will no
longer have a share in all that is done under the sun.
(vv. 4–6)*

It's better to be alive than dead. Now there's a brilliant insight, right?

Solomon is saying don't give up hope and give in to despair. Just because life is vanity does not mean it is hopeless. Life is a common blessing that God has bestowed on men.

Life is better than death because at least when you're alive, you know that one day you're going to die, so you can change your life and make something out of it.

In the last chapter Solomon told us to stay poised, do the right thing, and fly by the panel. In verse 7 of chapter 9, Solomon gives us three key insights.

*Go then, eat your bread in happiness, and drink your
wine with a cheerful heart; for God has already
approved your works.*

At first this may seem odd. Is Solomon telling us to bury our heads in the sand and ignore the tragic nature of life? Is he saying we should try to dull the pain with pleasure?

Again, as Augustine said, we are to translate Scripture with other Scripture. And in other passages in the Bible, we are clearly told not to get drunk and fall into debauchery. So what is Solomon talking about?

He's saying the same thing he has already told us. We should go out with some buddies, have a good meal, and wash it down with a little Columbian coffee and a couple of dips of Rocky Road.

Enjoy life right now even though you got laid off yesterday.

Spend some time with good friends. You don't know why yesterday happened. You don't know what tomorrow holds. Jesus said, "Tomorrow will care for itself" (Matt. 6:34). Right now, God will take care of you.

And God approves of your enjoying life. That's what the end of verse 7 means. Many Christians live as if it is a sin to enjoy life. But God created the world for us to enjoy. When Howard Hendricks said most Christians' faces would make a great cover for the Book of Lamentations, he was right.

It's OK to be a believer and have a good time. Do you know what the word "Eden" means? "Eden" is Hebrew for "delight." God gave trees that were good for food and a delight to the eyes. He gave woman to man and man to woman. It was wonderful.

One of the reasons God created the world was for our enjoyment. "For everything created by God is good, and nothing is to be rejected if it is received with gratitude" (1 Tim. 4:4).

Too often, Christians today equate fun with sin and misery with righteousness. But the Bible says that "In [God's] presence is fulness of joy; / In [God's] right hand there are pleasures forever" (Ps. 16:11).

Some of this confusion may come because people often only see one side of a biblical command. They see that God warns us to stay sexually pure, but they miss that He also commands us to enjoy sex in marriage. They see that God commands us to keep our speech wholesome, but they don't see that we should enjoy conversation. They don't want to be unequally yoked, but they miss that we are to bind ourselves to some good buddies and have a good time.

I think some Christians try to make themselves feel safe by keeping all the rules. They are frightened by life and by their freedom in Christ. They haven't yet understood that obedience to God does not alienate them from the delights of life. In fact, loving God only enhances our experience of real pleasure.

Let your clothes be white all the time, and let not oil
be lacking on your head. (v. 8)

If you were going to a feast in Solomon's time, you would wear white clothes and anoint your head with oil. Solomon is telling us to party. Solomon is saying to enjoy life as much as you can.

Enjoy life with the woman whom you love all the days
of your fleeting life which He has given to you under
the sun; for this is your reward in life, and in your toil
in which you have labored under the sun. (v. 9)

Man, enjoy your wife. Woman, enjoy your husband. Even though life is fleeting, enjoy your family and your kids. Isn't that some good counsel? Don't let today be darkened by the fact that you don't know everything. Enjoy right now.

A few weeks from now, I'm going to meet my best buddy from high school at the airport. We are going to drive down to Waco, Texas, and go to our thirtieth high school reunion. I'm looking forward to it.

This summer my wife and I are going to fly to Cape Cod. I will rent a car, and we'll drive to the place where my son plays in the Cape Cod League. We'll stay in a little bungalow on the beach. Before the sun comes up, I'll get up and go to this place called The White Hen and drink some terrific coffee and watch the dawn. Then I'll put on my running clothes and run up one of the most beautiful paths you've ever seen. I hope the world doesn't end. Maybe it will, but if it doesn't, I'm sure going to enjoy Cape Cod.

September will be dove season. My brother Bob and I will get a case of Dr Pepper from Dublin, Texas, and chill it down. The authentic Dr Pepper comes from Dublin where they make it with real sugar, not that corn syrup. Dublin Dr Pepper is real Dr Pepper like the disciples used to drink. We'll get a couple of boxes of shells and sit along a fence row by a mesquite tree. Bob and I will have the best time together, waiting for the birds to come in.

I am enjoying my life right now.

Why is this perspective so important? The other day I counseled a young, handsome guy in our church. He's healthy and doesn't have any bald spots. He's married to a lovely woman and has two wonderful little boys.

He is about to throw it all away by being harsh and cruel to his wife.

I looked at him and asked him how old he was. He told me he was thirty-four. Here is this young guy who is risking everything good in his life because he can't keep his angry mouth shut. I told him he needed to deal with his hostility and not squander his life through stupidity and sin.

You only get one go-around. I want to live well and then die with a big smile on my face that the mortician will have to carve off.

Whatever your hand finds to do, verily, do it with all your might; for there is no activity or planning or wisdom in Sheol where you are going. (v. 10)

Solomon says this is your only chance on this planet, so do what you do well. Note the progression in these verses: activity, planning, and wisdom. Wisdom is the ability to see. Planning is the ability to organize. Activity is the ability to initiate, persevere, and accomplish goals. Men and women are made to envision, to plan, and to do. God told Adam to enjoy life and cultivate the garden—He gave him work to do (and this is before the Fall). Solomon says that work is one of the areas that we can enjoy.

Paul emphasized this when he said, "Whatever you do, do your work heartily, as for the Lord rather than for men" (Col. 3:23). Work hard, be loyal, and do a good job. Do so well at your work that the company can't imagine life without you. Create something worthwhile with your life.

I committed myself to these ideas in my first job. I worked the cash register at a little convenience store called Keno's. I looked around the store and asked myself what I could do to be the best employee for the glory of God.

I committed to turn that store into the cleanest convenience store in the entire Western Hemisphere. I mean, it was clean. I would remove the goods from the shelves and dust them, and I organized everything in the store to make it look neat and orderly. I was making a $1.40 an hour, but I was really doing it for God.

When I graduated from college, the owner tried everything he could to keep me there. I thought he was going to adopt me.

That summer I took a job in Waco, Texas, for Ideal Aluminum as a sill maker. I took a big sheet of aluminum and made sills for the tops of windows. I committed myself to be the greatest sill cutter that ever lived. I arranged my sills in the assembly line cart so they were perfectly symmetrical. They were things of beauty. I cleaned my work area and polished my machine when I wasn't cutting. I took an air jet and blew away all the dust and metal filings.

And whenever a prospective investor visited the plant, guess where he was brought? By my sill machine. When I was ready to move on, they tried everything they could to keep me at Ideal Aluminum because I tried hard to do a good job.

I love to build and create even today. My wife and I just bought five acres of land. It's fun just to go out with a chain saw and work to shape that land.

It doesn't matter if you are working on an assembly line, at a convenience store, in an office, or out on the land; do your work well before the Lord. If you can't, then quit and go find a place where you can. Pour yourself into it and be the greatest at whatever you do.

You also need to work with wisdom. If you are just working to be successful and wealthy, you could be in for a rude awakening.

I again saw under the sun that the race is not to the swift, and the battle is not to the warriors, and neither is bread to the wise, nor wealth to the discerning, nor favor to men of ability; for time and chance overtake them all. (v. 11)

Work hard, but with an asterisk. Even great natural abilities and hard work don't guarantee success. Life is unpredictable; there isn't any formula you can use that will automatically produce a certain outcome. Time and chance overtake them all.

Consider Bo Jackson. He was one of the greatest athletes of our generation. An All-Pro NFL football player and a Major League All-Star baseball player, Bo Jackson was a marvel to watch. In 1991, he was at the height of his career and the prime of his powers. He was disciplined, determined, and focused.

Despite his natural gifts and hard work, on January 13, 1991, he was tackled from the side while running down the sidelines for the Oakland Raiders. Bo injured his hip and had to be helped from the field. Within a year he was forced to undergo hip replacement surgery, and though he returned briefly to baseball, his career was essentially over. Time and chance overtake them all.

Jim Elliot focused his life on becoming a missionary. He prepared and organized himself for years before moving to work with Indian tribes in Ecuador. After only four years on the mission field, he and four other men were killed by the Auca Indians during an attempt to approach them with the gospel. This righteous man was cut down in the prime of his life.

In business you see this principle of chance all the time. You work hard on a promising project and think the sale is in the bag. Months and months of effort go into it, along with dozens of letters and phone calls. Then right before the deal is signed, something happens and the whole plan falls through.

The next week, someone calls out of the blue, and you make a sale in less than an hour to a customer you have never talked to before. Time and chance overtake them all.

Who is the biggest guy in the Bible? Goliath. But he was killed by a boy with a sling. Who is the wealthiest man in the Bible? Solomon. But his life was a disaster. Who's the fastest guy in the Bible? Joab's brother. But he chased a guy who was bigger than him and ended up being run through by a spear. Who's the handsomest fellow in the Bible? David's son Absalom, of whom it was said that there wasn't a flaw in him from the bottom of his foot to the top of his head. He died hanging from a tree.

The people with the greatest gifts often end up with the most tragic endings because they're not wise. So enjoy your life and work hard. But don't think that your natural abilities will give you automatic success.

> *Moreover, man does not know his time: like fish caught in a treacherous net, and birds trapped in a snare, so the sons of men are ensnared at an evil time when it suddenly falls on them. (v. 12)*

God will rudely interrupt your life at very inconvenient times. His timing may be perfect for Him, but it often doesn't seem perfect to us. He has a way of making mincemeat of our plans.

If you don't believe me, try this. Take out a sheet of paper and date it. Now write down all the major things you believe are going to happen in the next year—the projects, trips, goals, events, and so on. Now save the paper for a year, then reread it and see how many of those things actually happened.

It's wonderful to plan; just don't love your plan more than you love God. Only one thing is certain about a plan; it won't work exactly like you expected it to. Do right and be wise but be ready to flex.

> *Also this I came to see as wisdom under the sun, and it impressed me. There was a small city with few men in it and a great king came to it, surrounded it, and constructed large siegeworks against it. But there was found in it a poor wise man and he delivered the city by his wisdom. Yet no one remembered that poor man. (vv. 13–15)*

Give me a wise man over a powerful man any day. A person who is not that brilliant or talented but loves the Bible, has a humble heart, and is willing to obey God will accomplish great things. Wisdom will whip power every single time.

Have you had your twentieth or thirtieth high school reunions? It's interesting to see how time catches up to the party animals. They've ridden hard and look pretty bad. They're not so cute anymore. But all the guys and girls who had the presence of mind to be honest, clean, holy, loving, and devoted look great and are wonderfully stable. Wisdom wins out in the end.

However, the text ends on a minor note. If you do have wisdom, don't think anyone will notice. The poor man who delivered his city was forgotten. How unjust! How unfair! In this world, you will never receive the recognition and appreciation you deserve.

> *So I said, "Wisdom is better than strength." But the wisdom of the poor man is despised and his words are not heeded. The words of the wise heard in quietness are better than the shouting of a ruler among fools. Wisdom is better than weapons of war, but one sinner destroys much good. (vv. 16–18)*

Even if you are wise, most people won't care. If you commit yourself to walking with God and serving Him, God will be pleased and you will have great joy. But a lot of people will think you are missing out on life. That's the way it is.

Injustice destroys righteousness all the time in this world. That's one of the reasons we hope for a better one. And Jesus Christ is the key to our new life.

Do you know Him? Do you know for certain that if you died tonight you would go to heaven and be in the presence of God? The only way we can be sure of that is if God has forgiven our sin. And we can be forgiven because His justice was satisfied at Calvary where Jesus died.

We need absolute, divine perfection to get into heaven. That perfection comes as a gift, earned by the life and the holiness of Jesus. Through Jesus' life and death, God can take away our sin and provide us with the righteousness that satisfies His holiness.

Have you asked God to forgive you and surrendered your life to Christ in repentance and faith? Let me encourage you to deal with this issue right now.

Unless you have a relationship with Christ, you will never be able to make sense of the world. You'll be like the writer in Psalm 73 who says he was "envious of the arrogant" when "he saw the prosperity of the wicked." If you evaluate this world based on the here and now, you'll be frustrated, confused, and depressed.

But once you know God through Jesus Christ, you'll realize that there is something beyond this world. In Psalm 73, the writer says that when he worshiped God, he understood that the wicked who were succeeding now were going to lose in the end.

Even though this world may not applaud wisdom now, when all is said and done, it's what will carry you through the inequities of life. Revere God, learn His Word, and obey Him in a holy, enjoyable life.

These are incredibly practical ideas. Enjoy life and work hard with wisdom and holiness, realizing that no one cares about it but God Himself. Hold on to these ideas simply because they are true. Even in difficult times, remember that your day will come.

For Discussion and Application

1. Why do you think Solomon recycles his argument about every man having to face the reality of death? Has this reality really hit you? Why or why not?

2. How does Solomon's teaching in this section relate to the teaching of Christ in the Sermon on the Mount found in Matthew 5 through 7?

3. What does the phrase "work hard, but with an asterisk" mean? Do you have this kind of perspective on your work? Why or why not?

4. Does it ever bother you that when you are wise, no one notices or cares? Why or why not?

CHAPTER 10

The Excellence
of Wisdom

ECCLESIASTES 10:1–20

How Can I Make It in a World Where
Ungodly People Prosper and the Righteous Suffer?

Sometimes I can identify with Solomon. Quite often I'll be asked
to speak at high school graduations. This gives me a chance to
talk to young men and women who are about to embark on life
without parental supervision. They have had many different
messages pumped into their minds. A lot of them are talented
and skilled. Some of them are good athletes. Some of them are
handsome or beautiful. But if you were to ask them what they
can depend on in life, very few of them would put wisdom at
the top of the list.

So whenever I get my twenty minutes to undo eighteen years
of peer pressure and institutionalized misinformation, I try to
show them that wisdom is the only thing that will carry them
through life. Even if they are talented, skilled, and attractive, if
they don't have the ability to recognize the sovereignty of God,

An Outline of Ecclesiastes
Following the Logic of Solomon
VI. Be Courageous in Life: 8:1–12:8
   Be bold in doing right even if you're not rewarded (8:1–10:20).

the diligence to seek Him, and the humility to honor Him, they'll end up as failures because of a lack of wisdom.

Dr. James Dobson once said that the greatest lesson you can teach a child is that life is loaded and she can hurt herself very deeply without the ability to make key decisions. We make truly major decisions about five or six times in our lives. At those times, we can either leap to a higher level or crater our lives. A good decision won't come through any innate ability; it will come through recognizing the supremacy of God, learning His Word, and submitting yourself to Him. This is what Solomon calls wisdom.

All of chapter 10 is Solomon's baccalaureate message to the human race. He is pleading with us to be wise as we enjoy life, our families, and our work.

Dead flies make a perfumer's oil stink, so a little fool-ishness is weightier than wisdom and honor. A wise man's heart directs him toward the right, but the fool-ish man's heart directs him toward the left. Even when the fool walks along the road his sense is lacking, and he demonstrates to everyone that he is a fool. (vv. 1–3)

It's an ancient science to be a perfumer. It takes a lot of skill, patience, and time to make perfumer's oil. Solomon describes how one dead fly in a bowl can ruin all of the perfumer's work. One commentator has said, "A little folly can display itself as mightier and more glorious than wisdom."

Ten thousand Christians can testify to the power of the Word of God, and one fool can offer pornography, and people will flock to the fool. I teach the Word of God, and nobody knows who I am. Everybody knows who Howard Stern is, and he is a classic fool.

Don't think that if you honor God, know His Bible, and live a wise life, everybody is going to applaud you. You're not going to have any popularity from wisdom. You'll make a great husband, a great wife, or a great worker, but no one is going to applaud you.

Peter went so far as to say, "In all this, they are surprised that you do not run with them into the same excesses of dissipation, and they malign you" (1 Pet. 4:4). John said, "See how great a love the Father has bestowed upon us, that we would be called children of God; and such we are. For this reason the world does not know us, because it did not know Him" (1 John 3:1). We shouldn't be surprised that the world doesn't like our wisdom.

Nobody will care that you fear God. Your life will be blessed, but you'll never get a movie deal. Happily, the Bible says that in the kingdom of Christ, a fool will no longer be called noble.

I have done a lot of teaching on romance and sex from Song of Solomon. We've distributed more than 100,000 audio and video tapes, and *The Book of Romance* has sold more than 30,000 copies. But guess what? *Playboy* magazine will outsell us in a day. I've got the wisdom of God behind me, and I'm a better man than Hugh Hefner. But nobody cares.

Do you see my point? One dead fly can cancel out a perfumer's oil. How many times have you had this experience? If you haven't had it yet, you will. A little foolishness can cancel out a lifetime of wisdom. Ultimately though, the fool will be found out.

In Israel the right hand was the place of strength, skill, favor, and blessing. David said, "He is at my right hand; I will not be shaken" (Ps. 16:8). The left hand was considered the place of weakness. That's why you hear people say, "I can beat you left-handed." It means I can beat you with my unskilled hand.

This is what Solomon is referring to in verse 2. Even though wickedness can cancel out and draw more popularity than wisdom, nevertheless the wise man's heart will direct him to the right. When it's all said and done, the wise man will end up strong, skilled, and successful. The fool, even though he cancels out much good and is respected in our pagan world, is directed to the left. He will end up weak, unskilled, and a failure. If you are not popular now, remember that the last chapter is not written. At some point, the fool is exposed for what he is.

Do you remember who wrote *Common Sense* and *The Age of Reason*? Thomas Paine was the author, and he had a huge impact on revolutionary America. But he also hated Christianity. He felt that people should do to Christianity what a butterfly does to a cocoon. He wanted people to put religion away as an infantile thing and fly in the glories of humanism.

Yale University experienced revival in the late 1700s under the preaching of Timothy Dwight, the grandson of Jonathan Edwards. At the same time, Thomas Paine died. Did he die as a revered statesman who was loved and appreciated? No, he died a drunk, desolate, broken, impoverished man. The news of his death and the circumstances surrounding it shook the student body. They saw firsthand that denying God and His truth doesn't work.

Let me give you a modern example. Darryl Strawberry was the number one selection in the 1980 baseball draft. His smooth left-handed swing reminded many of Ted Williams. It wasn't long before Strawberry became a star.

However, he also made foolish choices that "directed him toward the left." He has been convicted of tax evasion and arrested for cocaine possession, failure to pay child support, and attempting to hire a prostitute. He has been suspended from baseball three times and has entered drug or alcohol rehabilitation facilities on four separate occasions.

Several times he has made "miraculous" comebacks in the Major Leagues. But his final comeback was derailed, and his life was endangered by the addictions that drove him to leave his latest rehab center and go on a four-day drug bender.

Unfortunately, Darryl Strawberry is a fool. It breaks the heart of a generation to see someone with so much promise throw it all away because he lacks wisdom.

You and I know people who are just like Darryl Strawberry. They may not be superstars, but they are throwing their lives away by being fools. Solomon is trying to show us that wisdom is the only thing that provides lasting strength in this life.

> *If the ruler's temper rises against you, do not abandon your position, because composure allays great offenses. There is an evil I have seen under the sun, like an error which goes forth from the ruler—folly is set in many exalted places while rich men sit in humble places. I have seen slaves riding on horses and princes walking like slaves on the land. (vv. 4–7)*

If you find yourself in the minority when a wicked person is in a place of authority, don't give up. Stay true to what you believe. Your virtue and godliness will sustain you to the end.

Sometimes in the short term, life seems to be backward, and wicked men get the upper hand. Bad guys hurt good guys. When that happens, Solomon encourages us to hold fast to our position. Don't think that because you are a wise person who isn't getting applauded, that you can abandon your position.

It hurts when we see fools who are in leadership and authority. Do you remember the movie *The Sound of Music*? Liesl is the oldest girl in the Von Trapp family. A young Austrian named Rolf likes her. When we meet Rolf at the beginning of the movie, he is a submissive messenger boy.

Then the Nazi's move into Austria and take over. Rolf becomes one of the Hitler youth and is given a whistle and a little authority. Suddenly, he has more power than Captain Von Trapp. When you're watching the movie, it is almost silly—this great and powerful man is being ordered around by this runt.

In the end, the entire Von Trapp family is hiding in a convent cemetery and the Nazis are searching for them. Who finds them? Rolf. So now this young kid has them at his mercy. That's life. Fools often end up in positions of authority.

And fools end up rich. That's why Darryl Strawberry is rich. Here is a man who has been arrested multiple times and been through rehab over and over again, but because he can hit a little white ball, he has made millions of dollars. Compare that to a school teacher who loves her kids, works hard, has a master's degree and makes $35,000. It's just not right.

But that's OK because Solomon reminds us that wisdom still has the edge. When the last bell is rung, it's better to be a godly man.

> *He who digs a pit may fall into it, and a serpent may bite him who breaks through a wall. He who quarries stones may be hurt by them, and he who splits logs may be endangered by them. If the axe is dull and he does not sharpen its edge, then he must exert more strength. Wisdom has the advantage of giving success. (vv. 8–10)*

You can have incredible energy, gusto, and perseverance. You can go out and dig a massive pit. But stay away from the edge or you might fall in and break your neck. Avoid the perils of your own work. Be wise as well as energetic.

If you are clearing the stones from an old wall, be careful. All your strength could get you killed if there is a copperhead on the other side of that wall. It's not enough to have energy; you better have wisdom to go with it.

If you are a stone quarrier, be careful when you cut out a piece of rock, because it has to fall somewhere. Don't let it hit you in the head. Be smart with your energy, diligence, and talent.

If you're cutting trees, the same advice holds true. The tree has to fall somewhere, so be careful. And if you don't have enough wisdom to sharpen your axe, you are going to make your work a lot harder. Stop and sharpen that edge. If it's dull, you will have to strike harder and harder until you get out of control, miss the log, and hit yourself.

Wisdom gives you the edge. Even though evil has the upper hand sometimes, stay true to wisdom.

Alabama University coach Paul "Bear" Bryant was one of the first football coaches to watch films of his opponents. He knew that at the highest levels of college football, strength and skill alone wouldn't be enough. He wanted to find an edge.

He watched the films and tried to find habits or patterns that could give his team an advantage. More often than not, he would find some trick of the trade. For one of his bowl games, he noticed that an opposing offensive guard put down his right hand when he was blocking left and his left hand when he was blocking right. Nobody else noticed, but Bryant picked it out. He instructed his linebackers to watch the guard. They shut down the other team's offense because they knew the flow of the play.

Another time he picked out the fact that an opposing quarterback moved his right foot back slightly before the snap on passing plays. Nobody else saw it, but Bryant picked it out. He told his defense to watch the quarterback's feet, and they did. They had the edge.

It doesn't matter how handsome you are, how talented you are, or how much your inheritance is. If you don't understand wisdom, you won't ultimately have the edge in life. In the end, you will make a mess of all your wall building, quarrying, and tree cutting. At some point, being a fool will come back to haunt you.

That's Solomon's point here. Even though princes are sometimes put down and slaves raised up, even though life is unfair, stay wise because wisdom has the edge in the end.

If the serpent bites before being charmed, there is no profit for the charmer. (v. 11)

This verse looks like a random thought but actually is the key to this entire section. You've probably seen a snake charmer on television. And it's quite a talent to be able to charm a snake, but if the charmer gets bitten, his talent didn't do him any good. The charmer had the skill but he didn't use it. Solomon's point is that you need to use the wisdom you have. Otherwise, you may as well not have it since it's of no service to you.

It's not enough to know how to charm the serpent—you have to actually apply your knowledge before you're bitten.

Let's apply this idea to life. You probably have many areas in life where you know the right things to do. You could give a list of wonderful principles for marriage, parenting, money management, sexuality, friendships, and work. You know all the right answers in your head.

But that's not the most important part, is it? If the serpent bites, the person who knows how to charm a snake is no better off than one who doesn't. So the important thing is not just that you have the knowledge, but that you actually use it in marriage, parenting, and so on. You have to use your wisdom.

Our churches are filled with Bible-believing people who have mangled their lives because they were bitten by the snake. They didn't put their wisdom to use.

What about you? Are there areas of your life where you know the right thing to do but just aren't doing it? Are you praying with your spouse? Are you reading the Bible with your kids? Are you out of debt and using your money wisely to fulfill the Lord's calling on your life? If the answer to any of these is no, you need to put your wisdom into practice.

I recently taught my church's evening service and saw a girl who used to be in our high school group. When Debbie was in high school, she had everything going for her—a wonderful family, great knowledge of the Bible, boldness in the things of God, and superior natural gifts and abilities. If the youth group had voted, she would have been the one selected most likely to become a godly woman. I can remember looking forward to seeing what she would do when she became an adult.

But when Debbie turned eighteen, she went through about a year and a half of madness. She rebelled against God. She rebelled against her parents. She rebelled against the Bible and church authority. She started living with a guy and then decided she would marry him.

Like many women who are out of fellowship with God, Debbie was a sucker for a "Peter Pan" kind of man. She fell for a happy-go-lucky, airy kind of guy with a lot of little boy still in him.

Do you know what it's like to be married to a child? Debbie does now. She was drawn to this hurting man because the nurse in her wanted to heal the broken little boy in him.

But trust me, being married to a hurting child gets real old real fast. Nothing is more frustrating to a woman than a man who can't lead her.

They had a child, and Debbie repented and came back to the Lord. Now this young woman is a mother who has high hopes for her child. But her husband can barely hold a job.

She's now dragging 160 pounds of baggage around life—old Peter Pan. And when I was preaching in the evening service, I saw her. She was leaning forward, taking notes. I could just see her wheels turning. Meanwhile, sitting next to her was Pete with his hat on backward and his pants falling off. He has no business with this girl, but there he was.

What's the moral of this story? There is nothing I could have said to Debbie at any point in her rebellion that she didn't already know. She knows the same verses I know and could've preached a convincing sermon to herself to halt her blunders. She had the knowledge that would have kept her from being bitten by the snake, but she didn't use it. She got bit. If the serpent bites you before being charmed, you have no edge.

I don't care how much Bible you know, it's meaningless if you don't know how to charm the serpent before it gets to you. Life is loaded.

Wisdom is a whole lot better than any amount of brilliance, strength, or looks. But even wisdom is no good if you don't use it. The Bible is not meant to be studied like Plato's *Republic*. It is meant to be depended on like a navigator using a map to make it through an ice field: It offers constant direction and application.

Solomon gives us one more warning about the fool.

Words from the mouth of a wise man are gracious,
while the lips of a fool consume him; the beginning of
his talking is folly, and the end of it is wicked mad-
ness. Yet the fool multiplies words. No man knows
what will happen, and who can tell him what will
come after him? (vv. 12–14)

A wise person has a mouth that is gracious. He is loving. She is kind. They are gentle and humble and everybody loves them. People may not agree with them, but the wise are gracious. The Bible says that "a gracious woman retains honor" (Prov. 11:16).

Everybody loves a person who will put wisdom to work. If you're somebody who fears God, seeks His Word, and incorporates it into your life, I'll assure you that many people will like and appreciate you. They'll love you because you're kind, you're a good listener, you're gentle, and it's fun to be with you. You lift people up. The words of a wise man are gracious.

In contrast, the words of a fool wreak havoc. Discriminating people can't stand to be around him. The things he says range from the silly to the truly evil.

The fool opens his mouth and error comes out. And yet he keeps talking. No matter how he gets beat up in life, it never convinces him to repent.

Scholars suggest that the last sentence in verse 14 should be seen as a sarcastic sentence spoken boldly by the fool: "No man knows what will happen, and who can tell what will come after him?"

The fool pontificates and pretends that he has exhaustive knowledge about life. He fakes certainty to keep up the pretense of having his life together. It's called humanism. The fool says, "I'm in charge and there is no God."

But the fool's philosophy can't get him through life.

The toil of a fool so wearies him that he does not even know how to go to a city. (v. 15)

Solomon is making fun of the fool. He's saying that this person who claims to know everything about life's most important questions can't even find the next city.

Paul Johnson wrote a book called *The Intellectuals*. Johnson examined the teachings of many of the most important thinkers of Western civilization—men like Rousseau, Karl Marx, Leo Tolstoy, Jean-Paul Sartre, and Bertrand Russell. But he didn't just study their teachings, he also examined the way they lived their lives. He looked at how they treated people, their habits, their marriages, their kids, and their friends.

Do you know what he found? Every one of those people scoffed at God. They pontificated on eternity. They denied everything holy and presented themselves as the fount of all wisdom. But most of them didn't have the sense to raise a child well. They didn't keep their marriages together. They destroyed first themselves and then everything around them. Don't be misled by a fool.

Foolishness harms not only individuals and families but entire civilizations.

Woe to you, O land, whose king is a lad and whose princes feast in the morning. Blessed are you, O land, whose king is of nobility and whose princes eat at the appropriate time—for strength, and not for drunkenness. (vv. 16–17)

It's true for Russia. It's true for Germany. It's true for France and it's true for America. Woe to the country that has a king who acts like a child. A country is in trouble when it's leaders party before they have done their work. When leaders don't have the wisdom to focus on priorities and guide decisions with morality, a country is in trouble.

But the opposite is true. A country with godly, wise leaders is blessed.

Let me ask you a few questions. Which president said he could not tell a lie? Washington. Which president would walk miles to return the books he read by firelight? Abraham Lincoln—Honest Abe.

Why are those stories precious to us? They show the morality of those stunning leaders. Happy is the land that has a king who fears God. Blessed be the country that has senators who are not drunks and immoral men but rather followers of God.

When David became king in Israel, his first two official acts were conquering the Jebusites and then bringing the ark of the covenant back to Jerusalem. The ark held the law of God and symbolized God's presence among His people. David brought the ark into Jerusalem, put on the common garb of a priest, and danced in the presence of God. He exalted God among his countrymen.

Do you know what God's response was? This is the first time we see the promise that the Messiah would be a descendant of David. That's what it means to be a godly king.

Check out the countries that have renounced God for rationalism, humanism, atheism, communism, or Nazism. Russia hasn't done so well. France didn't do so well. Germany didn't do so well. And in many ways, America isn't doing so well either.

Solomon uses the image of a house to illustrate his point.

Through indolence the rafters sag, and through slackness the house leaks. (v. 18)

What makes a house become broken down and worthless? A lazy human being who cares only for himself, not the upkeep of his home. What destroys a country and makes it worthless? Foolish leaders who care only for their own interests and lack the fear of God.

Men prepare a meal for enjoyment, and wine makes
life merry, and money is the answer to everything.
Furthermore, in your bedchamber do not curse a
king, and in your sleeping rooms do not curse a rich
man, for a bird of the heavens will carry the sound,
and the winged creature will make the matter known.
(vv. 19–20)

In verse 19, Solomon continues his sarcasm. These men are the foolish children who feast in the morning. They try to solve problems with pleasure. Their only answer for the hard questions of life is to do more of the foolish things they are already doing.

In verse 20, Solomon tells us how to deal with the fools we encounter in life. He warns us not to inappropriately subvert the authority of a leader. Even in our bedrooms we shouldn't curse someone because the things we say will eventually get out.

Trust God and be wise in the way you deal with foolish men. Stay faithful to God. Use the wisdom He has built into your life. Even though the world won't applaud you, remember that the last chapter hasn't been written. The good guys always win in the end.

Do right wherever you are. Doing the right thing will always be best in the long run. This is the message of Ecclesiastes chapters 8 through 10.

What if you are reading this and know that you have done something wrong in life? Perhaps you've made some terrible choices and are suffering the consequences even today. Remember that forgiveness and restoration is God's major industry. He takes people who have made a mess and turns it into something beautiful. Jesus turns water into wine and makes it the best we have ever had.

Accept God's forgiveness and do the right thing now. If you haven't ever done so, turn from your sin and receive Jesus as your Savior. Jesus is the one who transforms us from the inside out and enables us to obey God.

Next, grow in your faith. Worship Christ in private and in church. Worship Him and see Him for who He is so your faith will grow.

Study His Word and listen to it preached. Let your confidence in the truthfulness of the Word of God grow. When you really believe that God is the only one who gives you hope, you will be able to do the right thing in tough times.

Then find a church and some solid Christian friends to walk with you on this journey. We weren't meant to walk alone. Get a few buddies who will stay with you through thick and thin and help you when you don't know where else to turn.

It's not enough to know the right thing to do, we have to put it into practice. Does your "doing" fully reflect your "knowing"? If not, ask God to give you the strength to live out what you know, so you won't end up like the fool.

Nothing is more discouraging than seeing someone who knows how to charm the snake get bitten by one. I'd hate for that to happen to you. Follow the wisdom of Solomon and let God's wisdom transform your life.

For Discussion and Application

1. Have you had an experience where one small mistake destroyed a tremendous amount of good work? What happened? What lessons did you learn?

2. If you need wisdom, what is one practical change you could make in your life to get it? If you have wisdom, how can you be sure you are putting it into practice?

3. When have the words of a wise person been gracious to you? What was the situation? How can you make sure you speak wise words?

CHAPTER II

Enjoying Life
with Contentions

ECCLESIASTES II:I–12:8

How Should a Christian Deal with
an Uncertain Future and Growing Old?

There once was an old fellow who loved playing golf. But he was near eighty, and his vision wasn't very good anymore. He always had partners with him when he went out to play so they could watch his ball and tell him where it went.

One day his buddies did not show up. It was a beautiful day for golf, and as he waited at the clubhouse, he got more and more upset that he wasn't going to get to play his round. Another old fellow in the clubhouse saw him and came over, asking, "What's wrong?"

The man explained his predicament: "I was really looking forward to playing golf today. But I don't see very well anymore, so I need someone to watch the ball after I hit."

An Outline of Ecclesiastes
Following the Logic of Solomon
VI. Be Courageous in Life: 8:1–12:8
   Be bold in doing right even if you're not rewarded (8:1–10:20).
   Be bold in living even though you can't control all things
      (11:1–6).
   Be bold in enjoying life, although death will come (11:7–12:8).

The second man was even older than he was. "That's no problem. I'll be glad to ride around with you. I've got twenty/twenty vision. I can see like a hawk. You just hit the ball, and I'll watch it fly right down the fairway."

So they went out on the first tee, and the old man hit the ball right down the center. He turned to his spotter. "Did you see it?"

"I saw it all the way until it stopped rolling."

"Well, where did it go?"

The older man paused for a moment. "I forgot."

Even the best-laid plans don't always work out—that's a reality we all have to face every day. But how do you live confidently and boldly when you're not sure how things are going to turn out?

I do weddings all the time. These brides and their mothers have every step mapped out with a battle plan. They have made countless checklists and thought of every detail. After all their preparation, the event should proceed with military precision.

Then they decide to include a flower girl and a ring bearer. That's like tossing a live grenade into their plans. Kids almost always bring the ceremony to a screeching halt.

That's the way life is—full of unexpected contingencies. Still, Solomon says we can live boldly even though life is unpredictable.

You have to live confidently. You can't hide just because life won't cooperate. Don't avoid blessings because of the concerns that come with them. Don't say, "I can't get married. What if difficult struggles come up between me and my mate?" Or, "I can't have children. How will I know they won't be born with Down's syndrome?" Or, "I can't start a business. What if it folds?" How do you live boldly in spite of all these worries?

Solomon tells us how in chapter 11 of Ecclesiastes.

Cast your bread on the surface of the waters, for you will find it after many days. Divide your portion to seven, or even to eight, for you do not know what misfortune may occur on the earth. (vv. 1–2)

The "cast your bread" line, though it sounds odd today, was already an old saying in Solomon's day. It refers to doing business in grain by putting it on a ship and having it set sail to be traded—casting it on the waters. You harvest your crop, send it off to sell it, and then receive back a dividend (hopefully).

Instead of putting your grain in a boat and sending it off, you could keep it and make bread. That would be a safe bet since you would retain control of your grain and your bread. But that's all you would have.

A farmer putting the grain on a ship faced many risks— pirates, shipwrecks, and unscrupulous traders. But the only way to get that financial return is to take the risk.

Solomon is saying to live boldly and let the chips fall where they may. Live fearlessly in a life you can't always control. If you live scared, you won't have a life. Cast your bread upon the waters.

Still, you have to find balance. Don't let your boldness make you foolish. You can't gamble everything because nothing is a sure bet.

Solomon warns us to divide our portion—the principle of diversification. Don't put all of your eggs in one basket. Don't gamble everything on one roll of the dice. Life is iffy.

I've met dozens of people who got excited about some money-making scheme they saw on late-night TV or heard about from a friend. They got caught up in the rush of emotion and risked everything, but then their plans didn't work out.

Diversify. Be bold but also be smart because nothing is certain. Life is full of surprises.

Paul's life is a great example of unpredictability. He wanted to take the gospel to Rome but couldn't get there. But when he was arrested after a riot, they put him on a ship and took him to Rome. Along the way the ship wrecked in a storm, and Paul was bitten by a snake on Malta. Finally, he got to Rome and testified to kings about Jesus Christ.

He fulfilled his dream, but how did he do it? By being the subject of a riot, then getting locked up, thrown on a ship, caught in a storm that tore the ship to pieces, and being bitten by a snake. Then he got to Rome.

God will get you to His destination, but en route He makes sure you go through things that force you to trust Him.

Solomon illustrates this with another unpredictable aspect of life: the wind. Sometimes it brings rain clouds, and sometimes it can knock over a tree. In Solomon's day, both of these things were good. Rain watered the crops, and a fallen tree could be used for fuel and tools.

> *If the clouds are full, they pour out rain upon the earth; and whether a tree falls toward the south or toward the north, wherever the tree falls, there it lies. He who watches the wind will not sow and he who looks at the clouds will not reap. (vv. 3–4)*

Sometimes it rains on your fields; sometimes it doesn't. A tree may fall south and be on your property, or it might go north and be on your neighbor's.

Both of these are blessings—rain for your crops and trees that fall for firewood. Maybe you'll get them and maybe you won't. That's the way life is.

Jim, the administrator in our church, gave $100 to the Dallas Opera raffle to support the opera. Imagine a man from Prattville, Alabama, giving to an opera fund. He did it to please his more cultured father.

You probably can figure out the rest of the story. He won the raffle and received a $50,000 Mercedes convertible. That's the way life is. It's the providence of God. You don't have a lock on what God will do. And the worst part may be that I'd look a lot better driving that car than Jim does. OK, so I'm a little bitter.

If you spend your time trying to outguess God, you're wasting your time. Life will never give you a perfect set of circumstances. You're going to marry a fallen person. You're going to have fallen children. You're going to get a job with a fallen employer. And along the way, you're going to get hurt.

Years ago, I had a young man named Jerry in my church who took his life at the age of twenty-six. He went out on a country road and shot himself in the chest with a shotgun. He got depressed because life wouldn't go his way. He made plans, but they never seemed to work out.

His daddy said to me at his funeral, "From the time Jerry was a little boy, he would separate his carrots and his peas." No matter how his parents combined the peas and carrots (as any good Southern Texan would do), he would separate them. He simply had to have everything his way. He wanted a life where everything was orderly and painless.

I'm sorry that life isn't like that. If you're always looking for that perfect setup, you are going to be an inhibited, frustrated, and lonely person. You can't live like that. You've got to let the chips fall where they may. Live boldly and let God be the God of grace. If you sink, trust God and pray. If you get thrown into a lion's den, trust God and maybe you won't die. That's what Daniel did.

My younger brother Bill has petit mal epilepsy, which produces moments of a semiconscious state. Even though medication brought his episodes under control, as a young man he would occasionally have a grand mal seizure.

We all worried about his driving a car. My mother called me and my other two brothers and told us that she didn't want Bill to live his life trying *not* to die. She was determined to have him live a full life. She said, "If we lose him, then so be it. But in the meantime, Billy is going to really live." This is an example of the sound wisdom I was privileged to grow up with.

Solomon is not talking about luck or coincidence; he's talking about the sovereignty of God.

Just as you do not know the path of the wind and how bones are formed in the womb of the pregnant woman, so you do not know the activity of God who makes all things. (v. 5)

Jesus paraphrased this verse when He was talking to Nicodemus: "The wind blows where it wishes and you hear the sound of it, but do not know where it comes from and where it is going; so is everyone who is born of the Spirit" (John 3:8).

Life is unpredictable and mysterious, just like the wind. We look at things that go on in the world and we don't have a clue as to what God is doing. But we have to trust Him because He is the one who makes and sustains all things.

Too many Christians freeze because they don't know what God wants them to do. They suffer from a paralysis of analysis. When facing a decision in their lives, they want God to tell them exactly what their choices should be.

Does God have to tell you what to do? Will God tell you what to do?

There is a difference between right or wrong decisions and right or left decisions. In the Bible, the will of God always refers to moral choices—decisions where one path leads to sin and the other to righteousness. For these right or wrong decisions, we can know the will of God. It's found in the Bible. We need to pray and pursue the path of righteousness.

For right or left decisions, God is under no obligation to reveal His plan to us. More than likely, He will not. That's why in Ecclesiastes Solomon says you just have to be bold and act.

Too often, Christians are looking for a no-fault deal. We try to do insider trading with God to get some information that will show us which choice is best for us. But God doesn't do insider trading. He does not reveal His plan to men.

In the Bible, we often see men who wanted someone to tell them the future. They basically wanted God to be their fortune teller. (See Ahaziah in 2 Kings 1:2–5.)

God won't tell you your fortune; He has already told you your duty. Don't call a 900 number to find God's will. Don't turn everything into a mystical decision about what you "feel" God wants you to do. If it's a right or left decision, pray about it and then boldly follow your heart.

Instead of withdrawing, let the uncertainties of life make you more faithful.

Sow your seed in the morning, and do not be idle in the evening, for you do not know whether morning or evening sowing will succeed, or whether both of them alike will be good. (v. 6)

The purpose of the sovereignty of God is not to cause you to lean on a shovel, praying for a hole. You know what I'm saying? You have to venture out boldly and let the sovereignty of God be your comfort, not your excuse.

Try lots of different things. You never know which ones God will choose to bless. Give yourself every chance to succeed.

Are you single and want to be married? I'll tell you what you need to do. Trust the sovereignty of God and brush your teeth. Pray, hang out where the godly people are, and let God be God. Do what you have to do and then trust God's sovereignty.

Throughout the Book of Ecclesiastes, Solomon has said that there are some things you cannot know. Now he tells us that there is one thing you can know: You're going to get old and decrepit and you're going to die. You can be assured of that. Aren't you glad you picked up this book?

In light of this fact, Solomon gives us some advice.

The light is pleasant, and it is good for the eyes to see the sun. Indeed, if a man should live many years, let him rejoice in them all, and let him remember the days of darkness, for they shall be many. Everything that is to come will be futility. (vv. 7–8)

Solomon says that in spite of the uncertainties, life is still good. It's wonderful to be alive. Even when it doesn't cooperate, life is still an amazing adventure.

When Solomon talks about the days of darkness, he is not referring to bad times. He's talking about the days when you start to get old and slow down.

Part of the curse of living in a fallen world is that we break down. I went out and jogged today and twice I had to stop and stretch my hips. Here I am at the ripe old age of just forty-eight, and I can't even run without having to stop and doctor my joints. That's the way it is. You just break down.

Enjoy life because you can be sure of something—you're going to get old.

You will not find a fountain of youth. You will not take your growth hormone and reverse the situation. I don't care how much Rogaine you use or how much you exercise, you will break down.

But don't let that fact make you miserable. Instead, start enjoying life right now. Enjoy your youth. There's an old saying that youth is wasted on the young. It's a sad fact that when you finally have enough wisdom and experience to savor and navigate life, it's too late to apply it.

Rejoice, young man, during your childhood, and let your heart be pleasant during the days of young manhood. And follow the impulses of your heart and the desires of your eyes. Yet know that God will bring you to judgment for all these things. (v. 9)

What does this verse mean? Remember Augustine's wisdom: Scripture explains Scripture—both in the immediate context, the surrounding context, and the theological context.

Obviously Solomon doesn't mean to get drunk, get immoral, and indulge the flesh. He has already told us the virtues of holiness and wisdom. He is telling us to follow our impulses and desires in the same way that earlier he told us to enjoy life.

When I was thirty-three, I followed my dream of running a marathon. I trained hard for a long time. It was a terrific experience, and I think God was pleased.

When I was about thirty-four, I had a great desire to go to Ireland. My family came from Belfast, so I always had a desire to see the motherland. Do you know what I did? I scraped some money together and found a friend who had been there. We flew over and took our bikes so we could ride across Ireland and Scotland for three weeks. Then I took a sleeper train to London and went out to Canterbury and spent three days there. I took all the pictures I could of the entire trip. The money's gone, and all I have to show for it are the pictures. I wouldn't trade it for anything. It was a wonderful time.

Have you ever been to Israel? Would you like to go to Israel? Save your money and go. I went there. I went for a run in Nazareth. I've been to Bethlehem and Jerusalem. It was marvelous!

What kind of dog do you have? Have you ever wanted to own a cool dog? Did you ever own a Jack Russell terrier? I used to read about Jack Russell terriers. Ronald Reagan had two of them. They will fight anything and are unstoppable rodent exterminators. In England, they take them on fox hunts, and if the fox goes into a hole, the Jack Russell will squeeze down in the hole and get the fox. Just pull the Jack Russell out by the tail and the fox will be attached to the other end of him.

A number of years ago I had a chance to get a Jack Russell and I did. I had Jack (I'm inventive with names) for seven years. He got an ear infection and the vet put him under to take care of it, but Jack never woke up. He was the second greatest dog in the world. I enjoyed every minute with him.

A year ago someone gave me another Jack Russell. His name is Buddy. He is the greatest dog in the world. I love playing games outside with him and watching him run. He is a little clown of a dog who sleeps at the foot of our bed and filled our empty nest.

Marathons, trips, Jack Russells—these may not be the impulses of your heart, but Solomon is encouraging you to find your own. We can be a lot more restrictive sometimes than God.

We ask, "Should I take this job or that job?" Which job do you want to take? Take it.

Someone asks, "Should I marry this person?" Is he a Christian? Does she love the Lord? Do you love him? If the answer is yes, then get married.

Another person thinks, "I live in an apartment, but I'd like to buy a house. Should I?" Can you afford it? If you can afford it, buy the house. If something is not against God's law, you can do it just because you want to.

God wants us to enjoy life. We don't always have to turn everything into a mystical decision. If you love God, do what you want to do. God will control things in His sovereignty.

Remember, though, that God will bring judgment. Make sure you play within the rules. God knows that the only way truly to enjoy life is to live by wisdom. You can't enjoy life outside of the context of holiness. Ultimately, sinful people can't have fun. Life bites you.

So, remove vexation from your heart and put away
pain from your body, because childhood and the prime
of life are fleeting. (v. 10)

Quit being a worrywart. You can't enjoy life if you're always scared. Live large, go for it, and have fun within the context of holiness. Do you want to start a business? Start it! Will it fold? Maybe so!

Thomas Edison once watched his whole studio catch fire, including all his plans and experiments. They tried to put it out but failed, and it burned to the ground. Do you know what he did? He stood up on the only thing left—a table—and told his assistants that they were going to rebuild everything in the exact same spot. Then he lay down and took a nap.

That's the way to live life. Get up and go. Quit worrying.

At the same time, don't do stupid things that hurt you. That's what Solomon means when he says to put pain away from your body. He's warning us not to shoot ourselves in the foot.

I've got a dear friend whom I love. He waited for a great wife, then married her. They had some intelligent, talented, wonderful daughters. He went back to school to get his doctorate. He completed it and got a great job doing something he loved to do.

He had a storybook life, but do you know what he did? He had an affair. And he got away with it. So guess what he did then? He started another one. So there were two women running around who had had relationships with him. Guess what happened? They met.

One of them said that she was having a relationship with a married man. The other one said she was too. The first woman said where the man worked, and the second woman said her man worked at the same place. Then the first woman said his name and they knew.

Never cheat on a cheater. The women called his wife. His life was so wonderfully blessed and happy, and he threw it all away for a few minutes of pleasure. It blew up in his face. It brought pain and agony. Here's some advice: Don't do that.

Do you have a bad temper? What are you thinking? Do you think you can have a bad temper and cultivate friends? When you go to a party, do you think people say, "Let's find the violent person and hang out with him." Nobody likes an angry person.

Are you a gossiping person? No one likes to be around you. Quit hurting yourself by your sin.

Are you living an immoral lifestyle? You are creating spiritual and emotional wounds in your life that will take a long time to heal. And you could catch something that at best will be painful and at worst could kill you. Don't do that.

Are you making risky business decisions that could sink you financially? Get out of them. Do you do drugs? That's dumb. Your body is a freighter, and it's all you've got to carry the cargo of your life. Quit tearing it down.

Solomon says to put pain away from your body. At the outset of chapter 12, he also says to remember God.

> *Remember also your Creator in the days of your youth, before the evil days come and the years draw near when you will say, "I have no delight in them"; before the sun, the light, the moon, and the stars are darkened, and clouds return after the rain. (vv. 1–2)*

Solomon reiterates the central point that he has made six other times: We should enjoy life with wisdom. You will get old one day, so enjoy life now but remember God in the midst of your fun. Don't become an old person who talks about what you wish you had done. Instead, be able to talk about what you did.

Live a godly life. Get up early and spend an hour in the Word. Read your Bible all the way through every single year. Read three great Christian classics. Cultivate great friends. Travel. Do the things you like to do.

A particular woman in Waco, Texas, recently took off from Mount Ajax at 10,000 feet to catch the thermals in her glider. She's eighty-one and said she switched to gliders from hot air balloons because they didn't go high enough. Enjoy life. Remember your Creator.

One day you will start to slow down and life will be more of a struggle. Some day the light will go dim. Solomon is using this metaphor about the sun and stars darkening to illustrate the winding down of a person's life. He goes on to describe how our bodies break down.

> *In the day that the watchmen of the house tremble,*
> *and mighty men stoop, the grinding ones stand idle*
> *because they are few, and those who look through*
> *windows grow dim; and the doors on the street are*
> *shut as the sound of the grinding mill is low, and one*
> *will arise at the sound of the bird, and all the daugh-*
> *ters of song will sing softly. Furthermore, men are*
> *afraid of a high place and of terrors on the road; the*
> *almond tree blossoms, the grasshopper drags himself*
> *along, and the caperberry is ineffective. For man goes*
> *to his eternal home while mourners go about in the*
> *street. (vv. 3–5)*

Do you know what these verses are talking about? Who are the watchmen that protect you in a fight? Your hands are the watchmen. Some day your watchmen are going to shake with the involuntary tremors of old age.

Who are your mighty men? Your shoulders. And one day they will not stand as tall and straight as they do now.

Who are the grinding ones that one day will be idle? Your teeth. And if you get old enough, one day your food may have to come out of a blender.

Who looks through the windows? Your eyes. And one day you will not see as well anymore.

I've experienced eye trouble myself. I bought a disposable camera for my high school reunion, and a buddy was using it to take pictures of the event. I asked him how many shots were left. He called me over to take a look. Both of us looked at the dial of pictures remaining but couldn't tell what the number was. We had about five people passing the camera around and straining their eyesight until someone finally put aside his vanity and put on his reading glasses and solved the mystery.

What are the doors on the street that are shut? Your ears, because you won't be able to hear anymore. And even though you can't hear during the day, you'll wake up at the least little thing during the night.

As for arising at the sound of a bird, my wife's grand-parents, Verle and Nettie, live way out in east Texas. As they got older, they began getting tired earlier, so they started going to bed just before sundown. Then they would wake up at about four in the morning while it was still dark.

Once, on the first day of daylight saving time, they went to bed an hour earlier by mistake. Verle woke up and saw that it was already getting light outside. He turned to Nettie and told her to get up because they had overslept. They got up and started scrambling eggs, then Grandpa Verle looked around and said that something was wrong. He realized it was getting darker, not lighter.

It turns out that they had gotten up and started cooking breakfast at dusk—just when the sun was going down. That, my friend, is rising early.

The daughters of song are a sign of joy and happiness. What happens when you get old? You get grouchy. If you are not careful, you will just get crabby.

Solomon also warns in verse 5 that you will get tentative and afraid. When you get old and fall down, you don't bounce back so quickly. You can become afraid to go out. So many physically overwhelming things can happen to you.

Do you know what the almond tree gives off? White blossoms. Solomon is talking about our hair turning gray.

When you get old, you're like a grasshopper dragging itself along. What you used to do, you can't do anymore. I'm just forty-eight and I feel it when I go out to hit balls with my boy. There are things that I just can't do anymore.

Solomon even touches on the sexual aspects of aging. In Israel the caperberry was considered an aphrodisiac. Solomon says things just won't work the way they used to. Even today, Viagra doesn't work all the time. Every one of us is going to get old.

Solomon says that we are all headed to our eternal home. Every one of us will end up in the grave. So he reiterates that we need to honor God and enjoy life while we can.

Remember Him before the silver cord is broken and the golden bowl is crushed, the pitcher by the well is shattered and the wheel at the cistern is crushed. (v. 6)

All of the items mentioned in verse 6 are associated with a well. Throughout Scripture, a well is a metaphor for life. But this well is no longer being used for drawing water. Someday your body is going to wear out. You will be nothing but a dry shell of your former self.

Then the dust will return to the earth as it was, and the spirit will return to God who gave it. "Vanity of vanities," says the Preacher, "all is vanity!" (vv. 7–8)

Your body will return to the ground. The molecules that make up your body will be recycled into the system of nature. But your spirit will return to God.

Solomon closes by saying that life without wisdom is vanity. If you think you can stop the aging process, if you think you can be a fool and enjoy life, if you think there is any hope for happiness apart from God, Solomon says you are a fool.

One day, when the curtain closes on the final act, judgment will come. Enjoy life now, live with wisdom, and honor God with every breath you take.

For Discussion and Application

1. Are you more of a cautious person or more of a risk taker? Think of a few examples. After reading this chapter, how might God be calling you to change?

2. Solomon states that your doubts make you work harder and be more faithful, yet some people are paralyzed by doubt and fear. Why do you think this is? Has this ever happened to you?

3. Solomon says that we should enjoy the life God has given us while we can. Think about the last two weeks. How many things did you do just because you really enjoyed them?

4. If you could do one thing differently in the next year, what would it be?

CHAPTER 12

Nails, Goads, *and* Glory

ECCLESIASTES 12:9–14

Why Should I Listen to What Solomon Says in Ecclesiastes?

Phil, a friend of mine, is a wonderfully successful businessman. His business has been growing for years. Phil has guided it through good times and bad times. He has helped a lot of people get good jobs to provide for their families. In his personal life, he has made great contributions to his church, to charities, and to the community. But do you know what I love most about Phil? It's his Bible.

As successful as Phil is by human standards, he's got a Bible that is held together with duct tape. It looks like it's been dragged behind a truck, because it's so worn out. There's every sort of tea stain, coffee stain, and tear stain on it; he has read the ink off the pages.

An Outline of Ecclesiastes
Following the Logic of Solomon
VII. A Creedal Statement: 12:9–14
God has revealed Himself to us through His Word.

But you know what? When Phil goes to be with the Lord, the item that his children will fight for will be his Bible. That Bible is the essence of that father.

There's a story about a pastor who was at the airport. At the metal detector, a security guard asked him, "What do you have in that briefcase?"

The minister replied, "In my briefcase I have a plumb line, a measuring rod, a hammer, bread, water, a crystal ball, a compass, a mirror, a sword, and my birth certificate."

The security guard scoffed. "There's no way you could get all that into that briefcase."

The pastor said, "Check for yourself," and opened the briefcase.

The man looked inside. The only object in there was the pastor's Bible.

Solomon concludes Ecclesiastes by giving us a creedal statement about the divine nature of the Bible. He tells us about the author, the book, and the reader of Ecclesiastes. In verse 9, he tells us about the author—himself.

In addition to being a wise man, the Preacher also taught the people knowledge; and he pondered, searched out and arranged many proverbs.

Solomon, the author, speaks of himself in the third person. He was wise. In Israel that description simply meant that he knew the will of God.

Verse 9 says that he taught people knowledge and arranged proverbs. A proverb is a truism that applies to life. First Kings 4:32 tells us that Solomon wrote thousands of proverbs to help his people navigate life. He didn't just rule them; he led them.

He gave them axiomatic ideas about the navigation of life. God was not trying to turn the Jews into mystics; He was trying to make them holy. He wanted them to live life as He meant it to be lived and to enjoy the life He'd given them.

Solomon wisely conveyed his knowledge of God to the people. Later, in verse 11, he says that these truths "are given by one Shepherd." Solomon recognized that these words did not originate with him—that the ultimate Shepherd of Israel was God. Solomon was merely a vice-regent accountable to Him. Here he claims to be something more than just a wise man; he claims that his words are given by God.

We have a term for God-given knowledge in theology—inspiration. God takes a human being and channels inerrant truth through him. Peter put it like this: "No prophecy was ever made by an act of human will, but men moved by the Holy Spirit spoke from God" (2 Pet. 1:21). In the Acts 27:15, the same word is used that connotes the wind filling a sail and controlling a ship. Peter says that the biblical authors were borne along by the Holy Spirit, meaning, God took human authors and led them to do what they never could do on their own.

The correlation between the written Word of God and the living Word of God, Jesus Christ, is God condescending to enter into humanity so that we might know Him. Jesus Christ is divinity who came to us in human form through a sinful woman, Mary. The Son of God reveals God to us. Can He create a man without sin? Can He override Mary? Yes, He can.

In Scripture, God the Holy Spirit works through sinful men to create a book without error. Can God create a book without error? Can He override Peter, Paul, Jeremiah, and the rest of them? Yes, He can. So the relationship between the living Word of God and the written Word of God is that in both cases, God reveals Himself to us.

God still used Solomon's human expertise. Solomon pondered, searched out, and arranged his thoughts. God took his effort and unique combination of skills to give us an inerrant record in this book. Solomon goes on to describe the book that he wrote.

> *The Preacher sought to find delightful words and to write words of truth correctly.*
> *The words of wise men are like goads, and masters of these collections are like well-driven nails; they are given by one Shepherd. (vv. 10–11)*

The book Solomon wrote is delightful and pleasing. Psalm 19 calls the words of the Lord sweeter than honey. First Peter calls them milk.

I personally have no greater joy than waking up at about 4:00 or 4:30 in the morning when nothing is happening. I get up in total quiet and put on a pot of coffee. If you want to know God, you need something addictive in your life by which you can study the Bible. I pour a cup of coffee, lean back in a recliner with my Bible and my pen, and I read. I'll get a good commentary to read along with my Bible and I'll just study.

Almost every day God blesses my heart with new insight. I think it's because I've got His full attention because nobody else in Denton, Texas, is up at that hour. He blesses me, I say, "Wow," take a sip of my coffee, then pray about it. It's me and the Lord. Sometimes I look up from my study and discover I've spent two hours enjoying God.

That is why I'm not just parroting old bromides when I preach and teach. I can preach the truth that God is showing me in His Word. It's a delight.

Solomon also says in verse 10 that these words are true and

correct. When you read something in the Bible, you never have to worry about being misled by it. God will never lead you astray. You can bank on it.

When I got out my trusty chain saw to clear the trees on my five acres of land, I had to follow the chain saw operating directions. It said to put so much oil in such amount of gas. So I did that. Then it said to put some oil in over here. So I did that. Then it told me to screw this thing down and every so often to tighten this and do that. After I checked all those things, then I could crank it.

When I followed the directions and cranked it, it started right up because the instructions were perfectly in keeping with the mind of whoever designed that chain saw. That machine worked just like it should work.

That's what the Bible does for our lives. It is God's instruction manual for man, and if you'll follow it, He won't mislead you. It is perfectly in keeping with the mind of its Author.

I was at a 7-Eleven last week and saw a guy walk in the store with a confused look on his face. He was from out of town and asked if anybody in the store knew a street called Redwood. I know that Redwood is a little bitty, one-way, cul-de-sac kind of street. Nobody knows where it is. And sure enough, nobody in the store did, besides me.

He faced me and asked if I knew where Redwood was. I said, "Son, you're in the right place. I'm an authority on Redwood." I told him that when I was twenty-three years old, I found eight hundred dollars in a wallet that had been dropped in a parking lot. Inside the wallet was a receipt from an eye doctor to a man who lived on Redwood. I went to the address on Redwood, gave it to a little old lady in that house, and made a lifelong friend out of her. Not only that, but I have other good friends who live on Redwood. I'm an authority on Redwood.

So I told him exactly how to get to Redwood. This guy sang my praises.

That's what the Bible is: true, straight direction. It was given by one Shepherd through men who worked hard to give us knowledge that is true and a delight.

Solomon continues his point with an illustration. Do you know what a goad is? If you are a shepherd, a rod and a staff are critical to your work. A staff is about six feet long and protects the sheep from a wolf. A rod is about three feet long and is used as a goad. When a little sheep gets off the path, a shepherd takes his goad and gives him a pop. It doesn't feel great to the sheep, but the shepherd does it because he loves the sheep.

You also use a goad on an ox. An ox goad is about six feet long and is used to poke the ox so he will stay on the right path.

When Paul's name was still Saul, Jesus met him on the road to Damascus and asked him, "Saul, Saul, why are you persecuting Me? It is hard for you to kick against the goads" (Acts 26:14).

The Bible is a goad. It will keep you from doing ignorant things. It also can be unpleasant. It can hurt sometimes. Yet David said in Psalm 23:4, "Thy rod and Thy staff, they comfort me." Knowing you're on the right path is a great comfort, and God's Word will definitely keep you on the right path.

Solomon also says people who master the words of wise men are like well-driven nails. When you entered Jewish homes in Solomon's day, there wouldn't be a coat rack; there would simply be a nail or a peg driven into the wall where a Jewish family would hang their most important articles. One of the names of the Messiah in the Old Testament is the peg that comes from Judah (Zech. 10:3–4). The Messiah is a peg. You can rest in Him. You can hang your life on Him, and He'll never give way. The Bible's a goad, and it's also a well-driven nail.

Long ago, my older brother Bobby had wandered far from the faith and found himself in a heap of trouble. He has a great mind, but everything else occupied his mind, not God. He didn't have a goad to keep him in line. He wandered and got hurt.

A few years ago, God reached down and touched his heart. God brought Bobby back to Himself, and Bobby started studying his Bible. He became obsessed by the Bible.

He wanted to know what else to read. I gave him a list of Christian classics. He began getting a bill from the library. I told him about Dallas Theological Seminary. He spent so much time in the Dallas seminary library that they finally made him a member.

Within a couple of years, Bobby had become a man of the Word. He told me that he wanted to share it with others. I explained that there was one place we needed some help, but it would be tough. He said he wanted to go where the action was.

So I got him hooked up with our jail ministry in Denton. My brother's now a superstar in that jail. He's got his own Bible study, and inmates can't wait to be a part of it. I get letters every year from guys in the Denton County Jail, thanking me for my church's ministry. They don't even know Bobby is my brother.

Once Bob's life had been changed by the Word, his wife also recommitted her life to Christ. She's one of the top Sunday school teachers in our church.

My brother was a limping, hurting, stunted man; now he is a well-driven nail. God can hang stuff on him, and he will support it.

What can God hang on you? What has He entrusted you with? Have you been faithful or have you given way? The Bible can direct anybody's life. Is it a goad in your life? Are you sensitive when God pokes you to yield?

Psalm 1 says that a man who dedicates himself to the Word is like a tree firmly planted by streams of water that yields fruit in its season. In whatever he does, he prospers. The Bible will make you rooted and strong.

It's the masters of the collection who are strong. Just because the Bible is inspired doesn't mean that it will help you. Even if you read it, there's no guarantee you will be strong.

Only those who have mastered the Bible are strong. They know it, they've struggled with it, and they've worked it into their lives.

It's not how many times you've been through the Bible; it's how many times the Bible's been through you. Do you have a time every single day when you withdraw and spend time with just you and God? Not you and a tape. Not you and a commentary. It's you with a confessed heart and the Holy Spirit working in His Word. It will bring you face to face with God. When is your time slot everyday that you're seeking to master the Bible?

In verse 12, Solomon shows us why many people never master the Bible.

But beyond this, my son, be warned: the writing of many books is endless, and excessive devotion to books is wearying to the body.

Solomon says that there is no end to the number of different ideas men will invent. You can read and study for hours on end and never exhaust the full store of human knowledge.

But you can be sure that none of these ideas will contain anything that is infinite, absolute, and perfect. All they are ultimately doing is adding to the errors of earlier generations. Man in himself can never come up with anything that will take the place of the Bible.

Even though it can be enjoyable to investigate all the ideas of men, it is wearying to the soul. This is why education cannot bring about rebirth. It has no power to create spiritual life.

I don't read many secular works. It's not that they're bad; it's that they're just eye candy to me. Every time I start reading something outside the Bible, I think about what I am missing: words of eternal life. It's like that commercial's tagline: "I could've had a V8." I could've been reading Romans.

Don't make the mistake of thinking that there is a plan B. There is no other way to know God than to immerse yourself in His Word.

We have now come to the end of the Book of Ecclesiastes. Solomon gives us his conclusions that summarize what we need to think and do. The climax of the book is found in verse 13.

The conclusion, when all has been heard, is: fear God and keep His commandments, because this applies to every person.

Another way to interpret the last part of that verse is "this is the whole of man." When all is said and done, fear God and keep His Word. That is the whole of man.

Charles Ryrie interprets that verse to mean that this is what man is all about. The Westminster fellows included this idea in the heart of the Westminster Confession: *The chief end of man is to glorify God and enjoy Him forever.*

The first thing that Adam knew after God made him was that he had been created by God. They had a perfect relationship.

Everything else Adam learned about creation, his work, the rules for living in the garden, and his wife, Eve, was born out of the context of his relationship with God. That relationship made everything else make sense.

If Adam had been shown anything of the creation apart from God, he could not have understood it correctly. The chief end of man is to know God. When he starts by knowing God, everything else in life makes sense.

Of course this is a part of what we lost in the Fall. Now God is no longer the default reference point for our ideas. That's why life can be so confusing.

I remember going outside on a wet morning and seeing drops of water suspended under a tree limb. At first they looked like they were defying the laws of gravity. Then I saw that a spider's web was linking them all together. When we try to understand the world without relating every piece of it to God, it doesn't fit together. He is the web that unites everything into a meaningful whole.

Thus Solomon concludes Ecclesiastes like you might expect: When all has been heard, keep His commandments, for this is the whole of man. But this statement assumes something—that God can be known. It assumes that God has given His commands.

God had made Himself known to the Jews. That is why almost every single verse from Ecclesiastes 12:9–14 mentions the Bible. It is the most precious commodity that God has given man. It is the revelation of Himself.

I told you earlier in the book that my wife and I purchased about five acres of land. It will be a place where we can grow old together. She's always wanted to build a Victorian house, so we are building one.

When I started clearing the land, I didn't realize that it had a pecan grove on it with about seven or eight beautiful trees. They were planted back in the 1920s. The problem is that hackberries and saw briars grew up around the trees and choked them—keeping out most of the sun and rain.

I got in that mess of brambles and branches and started hacking away at the weeds. Using my machete, I cut down all the brush from around those pecan trees. When I was done, I could see that the trunks of the pecan trees were huge, but the tops of the trees were stunted. They've never ascended to the heights and beauty that they could've reached because the briars blocked their light and stole their water.

That's how I feel sometimes when I talk to Christians. They are called and converted by God, yet so often they never really look like what they ought to look like. It's because they're covered with junk. Light and truth can't get to them. All their energy is spent on shallow-rooted weeds that curl up their bodies and choke the growth out of them.

Solomon shows us how we can clear away the brush. You don't have to assume the lotus position and be a mystic to know God. You don't have to eat some odd mushroom and have a vision. You don't have to find a cave and live in it. You don't have to go anywhere.

God has made Himself known in a document. To know God is a matter of diligence and discipline in the things of the soul. He has rigged it that way. That's the way you'll come to Him and that's what He honors. It takes diligence, discipline, and effort. What is your relationship to the Bible?

In World War II, one of the great terrors of the English coast was the German battleship the *Bismarck*. It outran everything in the English fleet.

Launched in 1939, the *Bismarck* was the most dominating battleship ever built. It displaced 52,600 tons and had eight fifteen-inch guns. It's top speed was thirty knots.

On May 24, 1941, a British reconnaissance plane spotted the *Bismarck,* and most of the entire British fleet was sent to intercept it. One of the first ships to reach the area was the *Hood,* which was promptly destroyed by the *Bismarck*. Only three of the two thousand crew members from the *Hood* survived.

On May 26, several more British ships caught up with the *Bismarck*. The great ship began pulling away from the British ships like it always did, when suddenly it began to zigzag in the ocean. Then it did a big U-turn and headed toward the English fleet. The fleet attacked with as many shells and torpedoes as they could fire, and they sank the *Bismarck*. Do you know why?

After the *Bismarck* destroyed the *Hood,* one of the British biplanes engaged and tracked it. This biplane carried torpedoes, which it launched against the great ship. One of its torpedoes just happened to hit the *Bismarck* on the rudder, causing it to lose its steering control and be at the mercy of the British fleet.

You can have all the speed, firepower, and engineering known to man, but if you don't have the ability to navigate, you are in trouble. You are at the mercy of the sea.

That's what happens to us when we don't know our Bibles. We get stunted like those pecan trees. And we find ourselves out of control and at the mercy of the enemy because we don't have any connection with the mind of our Captain.

This is why God made you. He made you to know Him as the foundation for everything else in your life. On the basis of your intimate relationship with Him, get a job, get married, have kids, and build a life. But every aspect of your life should be bound together by the common theme of your faith and dependence on God.

In our society, we have taken God out of the center of our lives, and our culture is falling apart. Substandard schools, high divorce rates, rampant drug abuse, and road rage—all of these have a rejection of God at their core. We are dysfunctional because we were made to live our lives out of our relationship with God.

You can't study marriage to learn about marriage. Study God. Then you can know marriage as He gave it. You can't study who you are by looking at you. Look at God, and then you can learn what He made you to be. You can't learn about kids by studying kids. Study God and learn what He says about them. You can't enjoy the universe unless you know the God who made it. Then you can study the universe and worship Him properly. You can't even enjoy a sandwich properly without knowing God, blessing His name, then eating it.

All of life falls apart when we don't know God. How do we know God? We know God through His Word. He reveals Himself to us in it. He transforms us from the inside out with it.

How are you doing? Are you immersing yourself in His Word? If you don't spend time with God, you will have to find some kind of saccharine substitute. You'll find yourself repeating the truths other people have learned and made a part of their lives. You'll end up acting like a Christian instead of really living like one. You will become a Christian mime.

Spend time in the Bible. Make it a higher priority than eating. Your body will die one day, but your soul will live forever.

In verse 14, Solomon closes with the idea that only God and His Word are eternal. All of us will give an account to Him.

For God will bring every act to judgment, everything which is hidden, whether it is good or evil.

God is the ultimate reality. All of us are dependent and contingent on something or someone; He is the only self-existent being. He needs nothing besides Himself to sustain His life.

We can have eternal life with Him through Jesus Christ. We can get to know Him through His Word. He is more interesting and delightful than any other subject we can study. We will never exhaust the depth of the character of God. There will always be more to marvel at within Him.

Once my wife and I were traveling through Paris. At the Paris airport we saw a Russian lady. She looked like she was in her sixties and she was by herself. She had a look of terror on her face. She looked at the people who walked by and said, "Detroit? Detroit?" to them.

She was trying to get to Detroit from Paris. At the Paris airport there are portals in every direction that lead to different aircraft. She didn't have a clue as to which one was for the Detroit flight. She looked at the portals and couldn't make out what any of the signs on them meant. She didn't know when her plane left. She didn't know enough to hand her ticket to someone and get help. She was scared and starting to cry.

My wife is a compassionate person. I was just going to say a prayer for the woman, but Teresa got up and walked to her. Teresa read the woman's ticket and found out that at one o'clock, the woman needed to get on an airplane to Chicago and then catch a connecting flight to Detroit. Teresa took the ticket out of her hand. She showed her our tickets, indicating that we were flying to Chicago on the same flight. The lady understood that she just needed to follow us.

For the next thirty minutes, this woman would not let Teresa out of her sight. Teresa went to the bathroom. The woman went to the bathroom. The time for boarding came, and our shadow was right behind us. Teresa walked her to her seat. Every now and then during the flight, I'd see the elderly woman look back to make sure we were still there.

We got off the airplane, and my wife escorted the lady to one of the airline employees and then to her gate for Detroit. We made sure she knew to get on the right plane.

Have you ever felt like this woman? Has life ever presented you with too many options? Have you ever been scared and felt abandoned or alone? It sometimes seems like there is no one who can help you get home and the clock is ticking.

The Bible can be for you what Teresa was for that woman. Whatever you are going through, Jesus Christ says, "I've been there." Just like my wife said to this woman, "I speak the language. I've been to America. I'm from there. Follow me and I'll make sure you get home." Jesus Christ says, "I know how to get through this. I've been to heaven and I'm from there. Follow Me." He knows and He died and He rose again, victorious over sin and death.

By trusting Him and clinging to the hem of His garment, we find life. You don't have to have great faith, but rather the simple faith of trusting Him with childlike innocence. No matter what you are going through, He is the Way, the Truth, and the Life.

The Bible can sometimes seem overwhelming. But the entire Bible was written to bring you to one point.

The purpose of the Old Testament was to show the need for the Messiah, the Lord Jesus Christ. He is the Son of God who came to die upon the cross. God punished Him for sins He didn't commit, so that people who placed their faith in Him could be forgiven of their sins.

The Gospels—the first four books of the New Testament—explain who He is. The Book of Acts shows you the power of His message. The Epistles—Romans, 1 and 2 Corinthians, Galatians, Ephesians, Philippians, Colossians, and all the way through Jude—explain exactly what He did and how we should live. The Book of Revelation tells us that He's coming back.

The purpose of the Bible is to bring you to the person prophesied in the Old Testament, embodied in the Gospels, explained in the Epistles, and anticipated in Revelation—Jesus Christ.

Solomon's conclusion gets to the heart of the matter. In a crazy, uncertain life, there has to be a source of wisdom that does not change and is never wrong. God has given us that wisdom in His holy Word. It's our task to love it, learn it, and live it. If we do, we'll find the joy that our souls have always longed for.

For Discussion and Application

1. Is the Bible a goad in your life? Think back to how you were a year ago or five years ago. How has your view of sin changed? In what ways are you different today? Has the truth of God been transforming your life? Think specifically of one or two areas where God has been changing you.

2. Have you known people who were like "well-driven nails"? What was it about them that attracted you? What characteristics did they have? How can you become like them?

3. Why is knowing God the most important thing in your life? How does knowing Him impact everything else that you know? Give one or two practical examples of how knowing God changes your view on another area of your life.

Epilogue

Jesus Completely Lives Out
the Wisdom of Solomon

Solomon shows us what wisdom looks like in the Book of Ecclesiastes. He tells us that loving and obeying God is the only basis for a satisfying life.

But if that were the end of the story, it would actually be pretty discouraging. I don't know about you, but I don't always remember the wisdom of God. And even if I remember it, I don't always do it. If I believed that it was all up to me to do it right, then reading Ecclesiastes would be a huge downer.

For the Book of Ecclesiastes to offer any real hope, we must have the power to actually put its wisdom into practice. Fortunately, through His life and death, Jesus Christ gives us the ability to love and obey God.

Jesus is the personification of the wisdom that Solomon describes in Ecclesiastes. "And the Word became flesh, and dwelt among us, and we beheld His glory" (John 1:14). A person who lives out Solomon's wisdom will look like Jesus. So let's review some of the key points and see how Jesus's life reveals the wisdom of God.

Even When Bad Things Happen, They Are Still under the Complete Control of God

Jesus was familiar with suffering. He endured a life of poverty and in many ways was an outcast from His community and family. He was falsely accused and tortured by evil men. His friends abandoned Him in His hour of need. Finally, even though He was the only innocent man who ever lived, He bore the full wrath of God against sin.

But in the midst of His suffering, Jesus knew who was in control. We see this when He says, "My God, My God, why hast Thou forsaken Me?" (Matt. 27:46). Even in His moment of agony, Jesus recognized that ultimately His sufferings were sifted through the kind hands of God. That's why He could then say, "Father, into Thy hands I commit My spirit" (Luke 23:46).

If we want to live out the wisdom of Solomon and Christ, we need to remember that all things come from the hand of God. His promise is that we will find our life when we lose it, and losing our life means that we have to suffer.

When Bad Things Happen, Be Careful to Watch Your Attitude toward God

In all the suffering that Jesus endured, He never grumbled against God. Even in His greatest hour of struggle, His words to His Father show respect: "My Father, if it is possible, let this cup pass from Me; yet not as I will, but as Thou wilt" (Matt. 26:39).

Jesus knew that everything that happened was ultimately for His and our good. The author of Hebrews says that Jesus was motivated by joy and hope: Jesus, "for the joy set before Him endured the cross, despising the shame, and has sat down at the right hand of the throne of God" (Heb. 12:2). So even though Jesus endured the ultimate "injustice" and evil, God turned it into the ultimate good—our salvation. And Jesus knew He would.

In the same way, when we aren't certain of what God is doing, we can still be sure that what He is doing is for our ultimate good. Even when we have desperate questions and feel that there is no hope, we can respond in faith, knowing that if God can redeem the suffering of Christ, then He can redeem ours as well. Our comfort is in God's character, not answers.

Don't Wait for God to Reveal Your Future; Obey God and Follow Your Heart

Theologians debate the exact extent of Jesus's knowledge while He was on earth. But it is clear from Scripture that in His humanity, there were some things about the future that Jesus chose not to know (He limited His knowledge).

Yet Jesus walked forward confidently into the future. He was absolutely certain of the Father's love. He knew that He loved the Father with His whole heart. So He followed His desires and let the chips fall where they may.

In the same way, we ought not to be paralyzed by fear of the future. We know that God cares for us. If we are seeking to love Him, we ought to follow our dreams and step out in faith to serve Him.

Bad Things Happen to Everyone, Not Just Those Who Don't Have Enough Faith

Jesus had more faith than anyone. His relationship with the Father was one of perfect dependence and trust. Yet Jesus had bad things happen to Him.

The world has been broken by sin, and bad things happen just because we live in a broken world. When Jesus entered our world, He knew He would have to endure hunger, thirst, betrayal, fatigue, sadness, and grief. His faith did not mean that He got to live a suffering-free life.

The same is true for us. Trusting God doesn't mean that we're exempt from suffering; it simply means that we realize our suffering has an ultimate purpose. Anyone who claims that faith can make all our problems disappear has never read Ecclesiastes or seriously considered the example of Christ.

Of All People, Christians Should Have the Most Authentic Fun

Jesus' active ministry lasted approximately three years. The New Testament verses record events that happened during only fifty-two days out of the life of Christ. During those fifty-two days, He was accused six times of eating and drinking with outcasts or of having too much fun. Jesus had a pure enjoyment of people and life.

Jesus didn't care very much for man-made rules and regulations. He knew that life is a blessing and that He should enjoy every moment. That's why He focused on the things He thought were important—building relationships and loving people and bringing them back to God. When He was asked why His disciples were having so much fun—why they didn't fast like John's disciples—He basically answered that since He was there, it wasn't time for fasting but rather for partying.

If you're not a Christian, there is a sense in which you can't fully enjoy anything. As mentioned in previous chapters, if you don't know God, you don't fully know or enjoy anything in His creation. You can't fully savor what life offers since you don't know who gave these gifts to you or why.

For instance, people who think that great sex will make them happy can't really enjoy sex. Sex wasn't meant to make you happy by itself; it was meant to be enjoyed in the context of a growing relationship with Christ and your spouse.

Jesus had fun because His life overflowed from His relationship with the Father. Find something fun to do and give yourself to it with your whole heart, knowing that it is a gift from God.

We Have to Do the Right Things and Let the Chips Fall Where They May

Jesus was courageous in the face of difficulty. He walked by faith in His Father and didn't let circumstances dictate His actions. When Satan tempted Him with "Turn these stones to bread," "Cast yourself down and let the angels catch you," and "Worship me and receive the kingdoms," He answered, "No. I will obey God."

Even though His loyalty brought pain, Jesus maintained His faithful pursuit of pleasing God. He knew that obedience doesn't always bring immediate happiness, but He never wavered in faith. Even in His final moments of physical and spiritual torture, He turned to His Father—"Into Thy hands I commit My spirit."

God will determine the outcome. It's our job to walk faithfully with Him along the way.

The Bible Is Our Only Reliable Source for Knowing God

Jesus lived and died by the Bible. From the earliest stories of His life, we see a commitment to and fascination with the Word of God. In the New Testament, there are 1,934 verses that quote the words of Jesus. Almost ten percent of these contain an Old Testament quotation or allusion. Jesus knew the Word of God.

How committed are you to the Word of God? How often do you find yourself thinking or speaking Scripture? Are you actively applying God's Word to your life?

Jesus used Scripture to defeat Satan and overcome temptation. He used Scripture to comfort Himself in suffering. He used
Scripture to answer kings and others in authority. He knew that
the Bible was a reliable source of truth to which we can entrust
our lives.

If you will devote yourself to Scripture, you will become
more like Christ. You'll be a well-driven nail and a master of the
collection who stays strong through the storms of life. In a
world that redefines truth every day, God's Word provides a
foundation that cannot be shaken. It's a great place to build a
life.

So be like Jesus and follow the wisdom of Solomon. Enjoy
life. Trust God. And live for His glory.

ADDITIONAL TOMMY NELSON RESOURCES

The Song of Solomon Conference,
a dynamic, humorous and candid seminar on love, sex, marriage and romance.

To schedule a
Song of Solomon Conference
in your area, contact:

Hudson Productions
800.729.0815
www.songofsolomon.com

To schedule a
Song of Solomon for Students
Conference in your area, contact:

John Wills
800.729.0815
www.sosforstudents.com

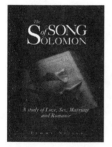

*The Song of Solomon:
A Study of Love,
Sex, Marriage
and Romance*

6-tape audio series
4-tape VHS video series
6-CD audio series
4-DVD video series

96-page Study Guide

*The Song of Solomon
Student Devotional*

A 25-day
devotional
for students

*Ecclesiastes:
Finding Wisdom
for Your Journey*

12-tape audio series
80-page Study Guide

*The Big Picture:
Understanding
the Story of the Bible*

256-page
softcover book
by Tommy Nelson
that explains the
biblical narrative
in an easy-to-read
format

Contact Hudson Productions at 1.800.729.0815
or visit our Web site at www.hudsonproductions.com
or write to Hudson Productions, 7160 N. Dallas Pkwy., Suite 360, Plano TX 75024